My 50 Golde
In Aviati

And my involvement with Aeroplanes

By Roger Creasey

A Retired Aircraft Engineer

First Edition
ISBN 978-1-913319-25-0
Printed in the UK by Book Empire

Cover Photograph
G-ARTA in Stockholm, 1971, by Lars Soderstrom

1

Contents

Dedication

I would like to dedicate this book to my Aunt, May Edith Davis, who sadly passed away before I completed my ramblings.

Harry

Hope this brings back a lot of memories.

Roger Creasey

Foreword

Review by a non-aviator! Mrs Christine Hilder.

Don't run away with the idea that this book is purely a retired persons nostalgic memories of life the way it used to be. Far from it. It contains a very factual account of one man's life-time ambition to become fully involved with aviation from its infancy to the present day together with accounts of many hoops he was forced to jump through to achieve it. All this interspersed with delightful anecdotes and recollections of some quite hairy situations.

As a non-aviator when I was asked to help proof read the draft I was prepared to become completely lost in technical data and terms and perhaps a little bored as a result. But quite the opposite was true, this book held my interest throughout and I could certainly identify with more than one of the many japes related.

A good read.

Acknowledgements

I have found many wonderful photographs on my journey through this book; however, I only have room for so many. Therefore I would like to thank the following for allowing me to use their photographs.

Ian Bagshaw, Ian Lucas, Bob Cooper, Dave Surry and Chris Anderson.

During the course of writing I found my memory of events from days gone by did occasionally hit a brick wall so I would like to thank the following for their help.

Fred Rivett, Jim Williams and the late Bill Richardson who passed away December 2019.

Our visit to the Croydon Airport Society back in 2016 bought back a lot of memories for me and their willingness to let us look through their old records was invaluable. I also want to say thanks for allowing me to use a Photograph of the Transair hangar that was donated to them by Pam Yates who with her husband Colin I had known for many years.

The Caterham Museum for confirming the details about the German Bomber being shot down.

Dave Lear who on many occasions has been on the other end of the telephone jogging my memory of more recent events.

Brian Buss the Aircraft Historian who I see at the Smallfield aviation meeting who convinced me to write this story and constantly asks if I am still writing.

Sam Westwell for letting me use The Pat Pearse story.

Thank you to Dave Thaxter for his encouragement and unlimited access to the incredible BCAL website without which I would have found this an almost impossible task. www.british-caledonian.com

My old Aunt May was the inspiration for writing about my younger days. Sadly she passed away before I could complete my story.

Christine and Malcolm Hilder who have spent many hours reading all through the text changing it around into a readable order so that non aircraft minded people will hopefully find it interesting.

Last but not least my wife Rosemary who at times despaired with my ramblings throughout when I have been dictating and she has been typing and on more than a few occasions has said 'is that the end of a sentence, or is that a new paragraph'. How she coped with me I do not know.

Finally without all of the above it would not have been possible to capture all the rambling memories of an old aircraft engineer, thank you all.

Introduction

Aircraft Maintenance in itself is not a very interesting subject. So, why have I written this book?

In the first place this is not a technical manual, you will not find out by reading this how to maintain any particular aircraft but what I hope you will find are some interesting stories and memories of days gone by. And for any of you that have been in the Industry, it will bring back memories of fascinating aircraft such as the DC3, Vickers Viscount, BAC 1-11, VC10 and many other Aircraft types that has spanned my 50 years in Civil Aviation.

My wife Rosemary has encouraged me to write this book and her efforts have spanned many years but I have always found a reason not to do it. I think perhaps the thought of trying to recall so much information (some 50 years' worth) just blew my mind and I wasn't sure my memory would stand the test. However, over the period of time it has taken to put this story together it has become clear to me what a wonderful piece of engineering our long term memory really is. I have found it relatively easy to recall people and events from over half a century ago, what happened yesterday is a different story. I must stress here that the stories I relate are not unique to me and if this book manages to come to print readers will be given the opportunity of jogging some of their own career memories and experiences of times gone by

My reticence was finally overcome in May 2015 following a talk I was asked to give to the Smallfield Aviation Group's monthly meeting, of which I am a member. At the end of the evening John Thorpe, one of the Group's organisers together with one or two members approached me, each who have published their own books on aircraft history. They kindly commented favourably on my talk and suggested that I should capture reflections in this way to avoid their eventual disappearance from history.

As we always say, Aviation is a very small world, but having said that the Smallfield Aviation Group has approximately 140 members in addition to which are the organising committee who are based in Surrey. Once a month the Group engage a speaker for the evening and these are mostly drawn from individuals outside of the Group. One of our members Fred Rivett he is now President of the Society, following the sad passing of Captain Eric (winkle) Brown, has on a couple of occasions been asked to give a talk about his Military flying career and his ultimate progression to Civil Aviation. I first met Fred when we were in the Air Cadets 450 Squadron at Kenley Aerodrome in the early 1950s. Fred was our Flight Sergeant so, as I say, it really must be a very small world for me to meet him again now.

My favourite aircraft, of which I have many, would probably be the one I knew and liked best, this being the Vickers Viscount with the Rolls Royce Dart engines. This aircraft was to us, at that time, so advanced and different from everything we had up to then been used to.

I started work with Transair at Croydon airport in April 1955 and this was an article written in the company review magazine in 1956 it shows how times have moved on since then. The article was called:-

"Kept em Flying"

Like every other aspect of aviation, aircraft engineering began in a small way.

Some of the pioneer pilots employed mechanics but others performed their own maintenance, in much the same way as the keen motorist attends to his car. As aircraft became more complex, more and more men began to devote their full time to the business of keeping aircraft airworthy. A new trade was born.

As recently as the 1930s, however, fitters and riggers could handle the majority of aircraft, the former dealing with engines and the latter with airframes.

The modern airline base, by contrast employs not two but a dozen or more different categories of tradesmen to keep its aircraft flying. Not only is the modern aircraft many times more complex than its predecessors, but it houses a great deal of intricate equipment, all of which demands specialist attention.

Today's fuel systems, for example, are a good deal more complicated than a complete aircraft of the 1914-18 era. A typical airborne radio installation of 1955 might cost as much as a medium-sized airliner of the 1920s. A course designed to familiarise tradesmen with just one aspect of a new aircraft's "personality" may last three weeks or more.

For every hour spent in the air, a transport aircraft will require perhaps 25 man-hours of maintenance. Time spent in the hangar is flying time, and potential revenue lost; consequently, when an aircraft arrives in the hangar it becomes the focal point of a swarm of activity.

The maintenance schedule sets out in detail the part to be played by every member of the team. Inspectors, foremen and charge-hands are there to control and co-ordinate the work, and to ensure that the standard of materials and workmanship meet the requirements of the Air Registration Board, the ultimate guardian of security in the air.

The fitter and rigger, still maintaining their friendly rivalry of an earlier day, remain at the heart of the team. But new members have been added and there is a specialist to deal with each of the aircraft's overhauls needs.

There are fitters to inspect and adjust engines; removing and replacing them when necessary. Fitters to remove, inspect and balance propellers and their operating mechanism. Engineers to maintain the airframe, the hydraulic system, the radio, the undercarriage and the autopilot. Instrument mechanics, electricians, sheet metal workers, the list is a lengthy one. In the background, storekeepers to keep the engineers supplied with materials, special tools and replacement parts.

But an airliner is more than a piece of machinery demanding the attention of mechanics. It is an airborne room, which must, inside and out, create a favourable impression on those who travel in it. In the ranks of those who "kept them flying", therefore, a special place must go to the remaining members of the team - the upholsters, the carpenters, the painters, the sign writers and, last but not least the army of cleaners.

Occasional tributes are paid to the men and women - involved in this business of aircraft maintenance, but for the most part the work is unseen, unheard and lacking most of the glamour associated with flying. For all that, it is vital work demanding much care and a deep sense of responsibility. Its importance is expressively conveyed in the words of the "Mechanic's Creed" written in 1941 by Jerome Lederer and first published by the Flight Safety Foundation, New York in May 1953, to which thousands of American aircraft engineers have signed their name.

"Upon my honour I swear that I shall hold in sacred trust the rights and privileges conferred upon me as a certified mechanic. Knowing full well that the safety and lives of others are dependent upon my skill and judgment. I shall never knowingly subject others to risks which I would not be willing to assume for myself or those dear to me."

"In discharging this trust, I pledge myself never to undertake work or approve work which I feel to be beyond the limits of my knowledge; nor shall I allow any non certificated superior to persuade me to approve aircraft or equipment as airworthy against my better judgement; nor shall

I permit my judgment to be influenced by money or other personal gain; nor shall I pass as airworthy aircraft or equipment about which I am in doubt; either as a result of direct inspection or uncertainty regarding the ability of others who have worked on it to accomplish their work satisfactorily.

I realise the grave responsibility, which is mine as a certified airman, to exercise my judgment on the airworthiness of aircraft and equipment. I, therefore, pledge unyielding adherence to these precepts for the advancement of aviation and for the dignity of my vocation."

PART 1

Caterham, Kenley and
Croydon Airport
Years 1940 –1958

Chapter 1

Caterham

I was born at 34 Town End, Caterham-on-the-Hill, Surrey, on 25 April 1940. The house we lived in was a 3-bedroom end of terrace and it belonged to Mr Rignall who owned the local butchers shop. My grandfather was a butcher and slaughter man; he rented the house from Mr Rignall. The garden was very large with two barns, one of which housed 20 or so angora rabbits and the other had cages for hatching chicks. We had about 200 chickens and an assortment of ducks and geese. At times granddad used to bring animals home to slaughter in the barn.

My Aunt May, who sadly passed away, early November 2018 just three weeks before her 92nd birthday, had lived her whole life in Caterham. She also lived with us in our house at that time. She told me that on the day that I was born, when the apple trees in both our garden and our neighbour Mr Swarman's large orchard were all in full bloom, there was a very heavy fall of snow, so thick was the coating on the trees that many branches were damaged and broken under the sheer weight. (Who says sudden, unpredictable weather conditions, out of season is a new thing?) There were 7 of us at the time living in the house; 4 adults, 1 teenager and 2 children, there would have been 12 of us but the 4 men, my Dad and 3 Uncles were away at War and an Aunt was in the Wrens.

This brings me onto a story during the night of 18 January 1943 when an RAF Beaufighter flown by Wing Commander Michael Wight-Boycott attacked a Luftwaffe Junkers 88 Bomber at approximately 05:00 hours.

We at 34 Town End were all in our Air Raid Shelter, that's all 7 of us when the teenager being my Aunt May then aged 16 heard a noise and being inquisitive looked out of the Shelter and called back to her Mum, my Nan, that all the washing was off the clothes line, unbeknown to her at the time, it wasn't washing but a parachute from the aircraft that had passed low over the Orchard and crashed in the Recreation Ground about 100 yards from our house.

Of the four crew, three were killed and one escaped but gave himself up the following night. The crew were aged between 20 and 22. One had a photo of his wife and family round his neck. My Granddad was in the Home Guard and actually went on patrol to find the escaped airman.

Bristol Beaufighter

Junkers JU88

I was educated at Caterham-on-the-Hill school, which comprised Infants, Primary and Secondary Modern. The school was on the corner of the High Street and Westway, which was approximately 200 yards from where I lived. It was basically all in the same complex and as pupils progressed in years they moved onto the next section of the school. The story goes that for approximately the first 6 months I was sent back home from school because they did not have enough teachers at the end of the War.

Chapter 2

Kenley

As time moved on I became more and more interested in aircraft and I used to cycle with my two friends, Peter and Tony, to Kenley RAF Station to watch the aircraft. We also visited Croydon Airport. We had books listing Aircraft Registrations and the idea was to identify aircraft by their registration numbers and cross them off, sort of train spotting in the sky! There was no sophisticated equipment in those days we had to strain our eyes to see the registrations as the planes took off and landed. We were also into making model aircraft; we would buy a set of drawings from a model shop and buy the balsa wood and everything else necessary to build the model. The biggest one we made was a glider, which had a 6 ft wingspan. We also made propeller driven types using elastic bands as a driving force. We would fly the models on a disused golf course near Queens Park Recreation Ground. We normally hand launched but also made use of a homemade catapult system. When the small Jetex engines came onto the market I then built, what I think was a D.H.Vampire using a Jetex engine. It took quite a while to build and on the day of its first flight we lit the engine and did a catapult launch, the aircraft went straight up and then straight down and smashed into pieces on the ground. What we learnt from this was that it's not quite so easy to build a jet powered model aircraft, so the experience was positive and we learnt from our mistakes.

When we were old enough the three of us joined the Air Training Corps (ATC). We joined 450 Squadron at Kenley Aerodrome. All three of us were mad keen and hooked on aeroplanes, and in the school holidays we would be at Kenley in uniform standing by the Hangar or Control Tower asking anybody and everybody if there was a chance of a flight today going anywhere. At that time Kenley had Avro Ansons, D.H Chipmunks, Taylorcraft Austers and Gliders. If we were not doing that I was dragging my Mum and Dad around different Airports to watch aircraft coming and going and I guess this is nothing different than what a lot of other young kids were doing, and actually do in the present day. My time in the Air Cadets with 450 Squadron at Kenley aerodrome did me no harm whatsoever. I think it's something all youths should do. It taught me discipline and respect for others plus I also had a great deal of fun.

In the Air Cadets we had drill on Sunday mornings which involved marching with a 303 Le Enfield rifle on your shoulder; these were quite heavy rifles to carry. Once a year, on Remembrance Sunday, we would march from Kenley to St Johns Church at the far end of Caterham High Street. These events made us feel special as people used to stop and watch us march by.

Evening meetings involved classes on navigation and aircraft recognition. I remember that I went to Summer Camp at RAF Feltwell in Norfolk. We were barracked in a hut, not under canvas. Whilst there I was lucky enough to get a flight in a North American Harvard trainer and did aerobatics, it was great, I've never forgotten it. We also had a trip to the decompression chamber, where they gradually reduced the air pressure to simulate pressurisation failure.

As I got closer to leaving school I decided I wanted something to do with aircraft as a career. I loved flying but I did not have the educational qualifications to follow this through. Apart from that, navigation is not my strong point, even today 65 years on my wife has a go at me about my sense of direction. So what did that leave me with as a choice? I must admit at that time I knew nothing about the mechanical side of aircraft other than they need fuel put in them.

In the meantime I wrote to Boeing and Douglas Aircraft Manufacturers in America also Vickers Armstrong & De Havilland in the UK asking for any photographs or literature on their aircraft (no internet then – how much easier it would have been). I received quite a lot of information especially from Boeing the American manufacturer and the more I looked at the information I received the more I was convinced I wanted to be involved with the mechanical side of aircraft.

Whilst at school we were taken out on educational trips to show you what jobs were available on leaving school. Some of our school trips had taken us to Industrial Factories off the Purley Way near Croydon Airport, but I soon realised that factory life was not for me. It was now 1955 and I would soon have to make my mind up as to what I was going to do.

As I would be leaving school at Easter 1955 my good old Dad said, "If working on aeroplanes is what you want to do as a career lets visit Croydon Airport to find out what Airlines are based there". During our walk around the Airport (you could do that in those days) we discovered 5 or 6 companies and we were hopeful that one of them might employ me.

Another memory I have is of the Farnborough Air Shows of the 1950s. My Dad would take me when ever possible.

The displays put on by the Test Pilots of the day were breath taking, hearing the Hawker Hunter breaking the sound barrier in a dive being flown by Neville Duke, the high speed fly pass by the Supermarine Swift flown by Mike Lithgow, Roly

23

Falks display in the Avro Vulcan were spectacular and what about Roland Beaumont and his English Electric Canberra taking off and climbing almost vertically out of sight.

Tragically John Derry and Tony Richards were killed flying the DH110. I can still see those two jet engines hurtling overhead and into the crowds on the hill behind us.

I completed my education and left school with a reasonable set of pass marks on my School Leavers Certificate. So that's that, now off into the big wide world, quite scary, as I was not yet 15 years old. What's the next step!

Chapter 3

Croydon Airport 1955 – 1958

This is now my story of how I became one of those dedicated team members who

"Kept em Flying"

My Dad and I decided that now was the time, during the Easter break to go and ask questions at one of the companies we had visited at Croydon. Dad and I arrived completely unannounced at a company called Transair. We walked into the Hangar and asked if we could talk to someone about the company. We were told to speak to the chap standing by an office at the back of the hangar who was wearing a white coat. He turned out to be the Hangar Foreman, Mr Ankers, whose job was many and varied including hiring and firing staff without reference to anyone else. He asked what we wanted and I think my Dad did most of the talking and told him I was leaving school this Easter. Whilst asking questions he asked how old will I be at Easter, I said it is my 15th birthday on the 25 April, he said "ok would you like to start work with us on the Monday of that week". If you're interested then you have a job starting as a Trainee earning £2. ls. 3d. (Approximately £2.06p in today's money) a week, start 08:00 hrs to 17:00 hrs Monday to Friday with a 10 minute tea break morning and afternoon and 1 hour lunch break making a 40 hour week. It was still a mystery not knowing what I was going to do. This made me feel on top of the world but at the same time very anxious.

So this was the start of my career in Aviation. I started work 2 days before my 15th birthday at Croydon Airport with Transair then, due to a whole series of takeovers or mergers Transair combined with Airwork. Then British United Airways (BUA) was formed from an amalgamation of Hunting Clan, Airwork, Transair, Aviation Traders Silver City, Morton's and Jersey Airlines.

BUA engineering at one point became Aviation Traders but soon reverted back to BUA. Then, along came Caledonian and we became Caledonian/BUA. Once again after a short period we became British Caledonian (BCAL). The final amalgamation into British Airways took place in 1988 and this was where I finished work on the 30th April 2005 having completed 50 years and 7 days of continuous service.

The Transair Hangar at Croydon Airport circa 1956 DC3 Aircraft in the picture include to the left outside of the hangar G-AMZH belonging to Mr Niarchos Greek shipping magnet and on the grass G-AMYW belonging to Hunting Survey before modifications, note the old cloth caps the men are wearing

After all my years service the experience, excitement and dread of that first day still lives with me, not knowing what I was going to do, who I would be working with or even who I would meet and what they would think of this 15 year old Boy.

On my first day at work, which involved a 7-mile bike ride from my parent's home at Caterham-on-the-Hill to Croydon Airport, I arrived at the

Hangar and parked my bike in the cycle shed. Very few cars were around in those days, there were mostly pushbikes and BSA Bantam motorcycles. I met the Foreman Mr Ankers who welcomed me and walked me around the Hangar to the Engine Workshop, which as I found out was to be my work area for at least the next six months. On our way to the Workshop Mr Ankers pointed to two Fitters in the Hangar and said "this is the type of person you will need to become, they are top notch fitters on the top rate of pay, £11 per week, one of those fitters was the late Bill Richardson who I used to see each month at the Smallfield Aviation Group meeting, once again "what a small world"; and the money seems ridiculous by today's values.

Then we went down a slope into the Engine Bay, which was situated, on the front right hand side of the Hangar. I soon found out that the slope was used to get the engines to and from the Shop and Hangar.

Once in my Work Bay I was introduced to the Engine Bay Charge-hand, Mr Peters who showed me around and said there was one other Boy in the Shop but he would soon be sent out into the Hangar to work on the aircraft. Mr Peters said it was policy for the new starter to spend 6 months in the Engine Shop before being allowed to work in the Hangar on aircraft. In those days fitters were "traded" as Engine, Airframe, Instrument,

28

Electrical or Radio (no radar as yet), so I was being trained as an Engine Fitter. Most people in those days were single traded. He then went on to explain what he expected of me. I was to call all Inspectors, Charge-hands and above by Mr or Sir and not to use any Christian names. I was to knock on doors and wait to be asked to enter.

Other duties included sweeping the Engine Bay, (it was called Engine Bay or Engine Shop as opposed to a Workshop). Sweeping was to be carried out twice a day and then before we went home, all workbenches and metal work vices had to be swept. The vices had to be closed then re-opened half a turn by using the handle, which is called a Tommy bar, and this must be left vertical. The "soft jaws" which are made of aluminium were used when working with soft objects and these needed to be left by the side of the vice.

Another duty included getting the teas and bread rolls for the fitters. This entailed asking all the engine fitters in the Bay and those working in the Hangar (approximately 25 people) what they wanted. The choices were tea/coffee, cheese roll or butter roll, cheese roll 2d, a butter roll 1d, these prices were of course in old money (£ s d), this happened twice a day, morning and afternoon. One fitter, Jock Stewart, always had one cheese roll and one buttered roll, he would then break the piece of cheese in half and put one half in the buttered roll. To his reckoning he then had two cheese rolls and saved himself a penny! Once we were organised with the orders and the money had been collected we took a very large metal tray to the canteen and picked up our orders. Then at 10:00 hrs a bell would ring to indicate tea break and the fitters went to the Engine Bay and we handed out the food and drinks, 10 minutes later the bell was rung to indicate the break was finished and to go back to work. I cannot remember either of us ever getting it wrong. I say "we" by whom I mean the other Boy John Titterrell, he and myself who took this task in turns.

Family life back in the 50`s was pretty strict, and for youngsters at meal times it was a case of no arms on the table, no talking or reading, these were the rules in our household. The only time the radio was on at meal times, if I remember correctly, was at 17:30 on a Saturday evening for Granddad to check his football pools. There was a deadly hush in the house and then he would yell out "no bl…y good". Then the radio was turned off and back we went to eating. I thought oh well going out to work must be much more relaxing, but how wrong I was.

Apart from the previously mentioned "duties" of sweeping and tea breaks, as a new starter, I came in for a lot of "stick" but no matter how much there was; answering back was not acceptable.

You have to remember that roughly 95% of the engineers were ex RAF or Fleet Air Arm; therefore everything was very disciplined with strict rules applying. On one occasion I heard the owner and Managing Director of Transair, Mr G Freeman say to a young lad in the hangar, "do you like working here?" to which the reply was "yes sir". He then told the lad to take his hands out of his pockets or he would not be working here any longer. Discipline sadly missed today! It was a case of do as you are told and no questions asked. Therefore, when a fitter told me to use my metal tool disc and go to Stores to collect a "Long Weight" off I went. The tool discs were small, round solid brass discs with your staff number stamped on them. They had a small hole so you could clip them together and hang them through a buttonhole on your overalls. You were issued with 6 discs and woe betides you if you lost any. My number was 36 although that didn't mean I was the 36th person in Engineering, it just happened to be the next set for issue. At that time there were about 100 Engineers including a dozen or so based in Berlin, that were involved in keeping the aircraft serviceable so that they could be used to carry freight and refugees from East to West Berlin.

So with the tool disk in my hand off I went to the Stores to collect the "Long Weight". After getting to the front of the queue at the Stores 'window' I asked the Store Keeper for a Long Weight. He told me to stand aside while he served some of the other Engineers. After about 10 minutes he said you had better get back to work, "you have had a long enough wait". You only got caught once on that one.

I have just read a book by Jackie Hymas called Spitfire Stories, one of her stories is about a lady called Kittie Perry, Kittie was in the Fleet Air Arm during the war and was trained as an engine fitter by a Petty Officer who, low and behold, told her to go to Stores for a LONG WEIGHT. This was exactly what happened to me, being told by Peter who was an Ex-Petty Officer to go to Stores for a LONG WEIGHT. When I emailed Jackie she wondered if this was a naval tradition.

Another jape involved a "Mag Drop". The Piston Engines on the aircraft were Pratt & Whitney 1830s, they had 2 magnetos per engine and when either Engineers or Flight Crew were testing the engine, the performance of the Magnetos would be checked, if the R.P.M dropped more than 50 rpm there was a "Mag Drop". At our stage of training we had picked up the expression (Mag Drop) but didn't understand the meaning, it just sounded important. So once again I was asked to go to the Stores and pick up a "Mag Drop", I did not question it. When I got to Stores all keen I was simply told, "you've been had" and cheers and shouts followed this. I felt a bit of an idiot.

Another popular trick was being sent to Stores for the H.T. Tester, this was a genuine piece of kit. The Store man would keep the Tester on his side of the counter on a table and hand you a pair of leads, which were attached to the Tester. He would then ask you to un-tangle the leads by "holding the metal clips". At this point he would turn the handle and you would get an almighty electric shock. Great! (I dread to think what Health & Safety would make of this today!)

There was a lot of fun. We had one lad Fred Dixon who was about my age who wanted to be a boxer. Two of the Engineers said they would be a Trainer and Manager for him. Lunchtimes the two Engineers, Jim Marks and Buck Taylor would cycle around the perimeter track while the lad ran and shadow boxed to their instructions. These training sessions lasted about a month and then he gave up. Some time after giving up boxing he decided to become an Escapologist, this caused a few laughs. On the far side of the airfield at Croydon Transair owned a brick built building which we called, the power house, it housed all our surplus spares that needed servicing and cleaning before being released to the aircraft. A couple of fitters would be allocated with three or four trainees to spend a morning at the powerhouse to attend to the spares. It was on one of these occasions that Fred got his hands tied behind his back one day by a couple of lads who tied his arms and hands through a metal milk crate. Two hours later he was released and that was the end of his Escapology ambitions. There was, however, one other thing he did but I will get to that later.

Chapter 4

Okay then let's go back to my first day at work. I was sent to the Stores to pick up three white overalls, one to wear immediately and two as spares. At the same time as picking up my overalls I was issued with my tool discs and given my staff number which was the same as the number stamped on my discs. On returning to the Engine Bay I reported to the Engine Fitter who I was to be trained by, a Mr Peter Mounce who was ex Fleet Air Arm. I soon found out how strict and methodical Mr Mounce could be, but on the positive side, it gave me the best grounding ever.

The Engine Bay was large enough to take four Pratt & Whitney 1830 twin wasp engines mounted horizontally in engine stands. The prime function of the Engine Bay was to produce power plants for installation onto the DC3 Dakota's, operated by Transair. To explain a "power plant", we would receive a fully overhauled engine from Fields Aviation at Croydon. This would be installed into a bearer frame assembly, which was eventually bolted to the airframe. To this framework we would attach a firewall and fire detectors. The engine would then have components fitted to it i.e. (carburettor, starter generator etc.) so that all the parts and fittings would marry up to the airframe.

We would always have one power plant completed ready for immediate fitment, one being stripped down ready to ship the engine off to Fields Aviation for overhaul and the other two would be in various stages of build. It would take a number of weeks to build an engine into a power plant.

Other functions of the Engine Shop were the combined cleaning bay, oil cooler test and overall facility. The cleaning bay had a couple of large tanks, one which contained clean paraffin and the other a deep cleaning fluid that had a terrible smell because the fluid was permanently heated. Fortunately this tank had a lid on it, the fluid inside acted as a paint stripper and de-greaser. The engine oil coolers, which fitted onto the airframe bulkhead just behind the engine, had to be cleaned and tested for leaks along with the thermostatic value fitted to the top of the cooler.

There was another room that was kept for cleaning and setting the gap of the engine sparking plugs. Each engine had 18 cylinders and each cylinder had two sparking plugs so over a fleet of 10 aircraft a total of 720 sparking plugs had to be worked on.

Last but not least was the area set aside to repair engine cowlings. This was manned full time by one person, a chap called Alex Sleep. He was quite a character who used to carry the cowlings like a Roman Shield and calling out "Hail Caesar".

When I first started working with Pete Mounce he let me use some of his tools. He had a very large wooden tool box, everything was laid out neat and tidy and at the end of the day he would clean all the tools he had used during the course of that day and make certain none of them were missing. Another reason for Pete doing this was to ensure that nothing had been left in the engine or on the aircraft that could cause an accident. It was suggested that I should save some of my wages to buy tools. My options were to buy tools from the van that visited the company frequently or to go to the Tool Shop at Surrey Street Market, next door to the Army & Navy Store. I still use some of the tools I bought back in the 50s to this day on jobs at home or on my tractor.

When I first started working with Peter he was in the process of stripping down a power plant so between sweeping up and getting tea breaks I managed to get my first 'hands on' experience of the work and I really enjoyed it. When everything was stripped down and the engine shipped away to Fields Aviation we would set about cleaning the parts we had removed so they could be inspected before being reused on the next build. Everything was inspected, including nuts and bolts. The inspection was carried out in the Engine Bay in the following fashion. We had a large (about 8 ft by 6 ft) flat surfaced table, which was covered with a big sheet of wood. On top of this we would place brown paper before laying the parts out, largest parts at the back and smallest to the front. We would prepare this work area by positioning a stool at the front of the table then lay a ball of string, two piles of labels one marked serviceable and the other marked unserviceable together with a pair of scissors to cut the string and then await the arrival of the Inspector. The Inspector's name was Bill Rollings, who was originally from Imperial Airways. He would arrive with his inspection torch and a magnifying glass, and cast his eye over what was laid out in front of him. Upon noticing the slightest bit of dirt or grease he would immediately walk away, saying all the parts needed cleaning again. He would advise the Charge-hand of his decision. Once everything was to his liking, he would sit and inspect it all and label the items either serviceable or unserviceable.

Once the inspection was complete we would start the rebuild. I will not go into great detail here; however, there are some details worth mentioning. The engine had two fire extinguisher spray pipes, one in front of the front row of cylinders and the other by the rear set of cylinders. These pipes often needed replacing and we manufactured these ourselves. To do this

38

we would take four lengths of copper tubing from the Stores each 6 ft long x 3/8" dia. We would then mark out two parallel lines along the length of the tube using a pencil. We were not allowed to use a scriber because that would scratch the surface. We then set about drilling 1/64" dia. holes 1 inch apart using a hand brace, no electric or pneumatic tools were to be used. This process made approximately 140 holes in each length of tube. We then attach nuts and a collar to each section and with a hand belling tool form a bell shape on the end for the collar to fit onto. We formed the pipes into a curve; using our knees and whatever else we could find to make a circle. Now there were two sets of fire extinguisher pipes! Well not completely finished yet we then had to hand-polish them with Wadpol.

All the flexible and rigid pipes that fitted to the engine would eventually be connected to the airframe, such as fuel, oil and de-icer; these had to have identification tape wound round them, yellow for oil, red for fuel and so on. Peter was very precise with this task; he used to say. "It is all in the presentation". Each piece of tape approximately one quarter of an inch wide had to be positioned "exactly" the same distance from the end of each pipe so that once connected to the aircraft all you saw was a continuous straight line of identification tapes.

The satisfaction came when the power plant you had just finished building was fitted to an aircraft and you were later given feedback that everything worked and there were no leaks anywhere. I hasten to add; you were soon told if there was anything wrong.

Back in those days most nuts and bolts were either split pinned or wire locked using 22-guage stainless steel locking wire. Nylon nuts of the type you get these days were very few and far between. There would be a maximum of one washer under the head of the bolt and two washers under the nut; it was preferable to have only one washer if possible. Although locking was achieved using split pins we bought very few bolts with holes as they were a lot more expensive than bolts without holes, as a result we needed to drill holes in the bolts to take the split pins. Sometimes when bolts went into the castings they had to be wire locked into the bolt head and this was quite tricky to do. If the bolt was fitted horizontally the bolt head had to face forward so that if the nut came off the slipstream would keep the bolt in position, it was necessary to make sure it was "head into wind". I believe this to be a throw back from the Royal Flying Corps days. All nuts and bolts used on the Pratt & Whitney 1830 were American standard (USF) at that time the British standard was BSF and BA but these could not be used on the American engines.

Well my training was going well I was still only 15 and a bit years old, and I do remember one occasion when it was my turn to sweep up, I was standing by a work bench watching one of the fitters splicing a rope, I was talking to him and at that moment the Charge-hand came over and asked what I was doing. I explained I was watching Mr Taylor splicing the rope to which the Charge-hand, Mr Peters said "your job at present is sweeping up and you will have plenty of time to learn how to do that job". As I said earlier, it was a very strict environment in those days.

As time marched on, still only 15 years old, it was my turn to have a spell in the Plug Bay, not the most interesting of jobs but it needed to be done and who was I to argue. This involved spending all day wire brushing the engine spark plugs and setting the gaps. My next job was in the Cleaning Bay to learn about paint stripping/cleaning and servicing oil coolers. This was something else I had to learn but the smell from the two cleaning tanks was awful and I doubt very much if you would be able to work under those conditions in modern times.

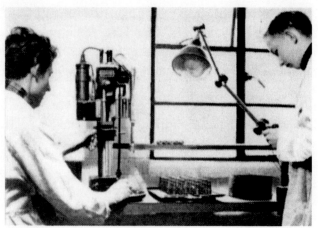

Roger in the Spark Plug Bay with Bill Ross left and me on the right with the brylcreemed hair

Wally Blackman and Dennis Turner working on a Pratt and Whitney 1830 engine, you can see the exhaust system being fitted and also see the fire extinguisher pipes that we made ourselves.

Ron Thaxter in the workshop drilling off a skin panel the arrow points to Ron

After completing my training in the other areas I moved back into engine builds again and on the odd occasion when I was completing a power plant build Peter and myself would take the power plant out into the Hangar to swap over any bits and pieces from the old power plant to the new one prior to it being fitted to the aircraft. Once that was done we would start all over again stripping down the removed power plant and shipping the engine off for overhaul.

My fitter, Peter, was the main stay of the Engine Bay. Most other engine fitters migrated back and forth to the Hangar but Peter got a lot of job satisfaction from doing what he was doing.

Chapter 5

As I was now approaching 15½ years old time was now close for me to be transferred into the Hangar. At the front right hand side of the Hangar was a wooden office that housed the engineers who ran the day-to-day operation. This was called the Flight Office and was manned 24/7 on rotating shifts 7 days on 2 days off, early shift, late shift and night shift. The Hangar operated on a day shift with overtime as required. I soon found out that overtime rates were good from 17:00 to mid-night, overtime was paid at time and half, after mid-night to 08:00 it was paid at double time. Saturday was all time and half and Sunday all double time. When you clocked in you were allowed to be 3 minutes late but after that pay was deducted and you had to make up the hours before you would get any overtime pay. This rule included going to the doctors or dentist, you were given no time off for appointments. There were some funny old hours worked in those days something else certainly not acceptable today.

Example 1: You started on day shift at 08:00 to finish at 17:00. You would clock out, go home and come back into work again at 19:00 and clock on. An aircraft would arrive from Lourdes in France and need a service check, so from 19:00 when you clocked back in until mid-night you were paid at time and a half, from mid-night

44

until finish at around 03:00 in the morning you would be on double time. You would then clock out and go home, get some sleep and be back in for 08:00 start again or you would lose pay.

Example 2: Start time 08:00 when during the day an engine failure could crop up and you would be asked to work a "ghoster". This would entail working all night and you would clock out at mid-day the following day. Although the engine change may be completed by 08:00 in the morning you needed to stay until mid-day otherwise you would lose a whole day's pay.

As I was only 15½ yrs old at this time I was not eligible for any overtime. At the age of 16 years I was allowed to do some overtime with the exception of "ghosters". At the age of 17 years I could do any amount of overtime but was not allowed to do permanent shift work, this only came in at the age of 18 years.

So with 6 months basic experience behind me, the day arrived when I was transferred to the Hangar. The engine fitters working on the aircraft worked in gangs of four. I was put on a gang with a Leading Hand called Jim Yeoman; his nickname was Titch. Titch was ex Royal Flying Corp and had been a Warrant Officer in the RAF. He was quite an elderly gentleman and I don't think anyone knew just how old he was. He was the hardest working, most dedicated person I have ever met. To show how dedicated he was, he had a growth on his hand, which was getting bigger and got in the way of his work. The growth would bleed on occasions so his remedy was to take a pair of wire cutters out of his toolbox and chopped the thing off rather than go to the Doctors, lose pay and put the job he was working on in jeopardy. More about Titch will appear later in my story.

Over the years different methods of control have evolved in aircraft maintenance. When I started we had Production and Inspection Departments. Production consisted of fitters, Leading Hands, Charge-hands, Foreman and a Works Manager and Chief Engineer. The Inspection Department, which was strictly non-productive, in other words, they did not direct staff, consisted of an Inspector, a Section Inspector, Deputy Chief Inspector and a Chief Inspector all of whom were or had responsibility to the Air Registration Board which later became the Civil Aviation Authority.

The entire authorisation needed to operate an aircraft laid within the Inspection Department; they certified the aircraft "fit to fly". Having previously said that Inspectors were not productive, this was not always entirely the case. There had to be flexibility and an example was when engines were being tested the Inspector would do the engine run up and he would tell the fitter this or that needed adjusting. Another example was when an engine or component failed abroad, fitters would be sent out with an Inspector in charge who would certify the aircraft for flight.

I soon realised that the Hangar was a totally different environment to that of the Engine Bay. It was a lot noisier with rivet guns and air drills being used all the time. Scattered around the Hangar were various workshops, Electrical, Instrument and Detail Shop etc.

Transair operated a fleet of Dakotas at Croydon, and we had two aircraft dedicated to carrying freight, which were completely stripped down to bare metal. The rest were configured, if I remember correctly, to carry 36 passengers. The fleet size grew from time to time and engineering played their own part in this by obtaining broken up aircraft, getting the parts shipped to Croydon and then, with great care and attention to detail, all these parts were brought back together to produce a first class rebuilt DC3, which when completed and certified airworthy by the Air Registration Board would be registered and put into service. I witnessed two aircraft being assembled like this namely G-AOUD built at Croydon and G-AMHJ built at Gatwick (I will talk about G-AMHJ later). These projects took a lot of man-hours and was never a high priority mainly taking a year to complete. G-AOUD was still flying in 2014 I believe.

G-AOUD as it was at Croydon before rebuild. Bit of a mess

G-AOUD when finished

Spares for the aircraft were acquired from various sources and not so strictly controlled, as they are these days. I remember very early in my career being told to jump on our lorry, a flat bed Bedford, with a few of the other lads and we went to somewhere the other side of Dartford to a big old house. Once inside the house we were amazed to find it was full of aircraft spares and tools. We took what was needed and brought it back to Croydon. I am not sure to this day if we had permission to do this or whether we just helped ourselves? On another occasion 4 Pratt & Whitney engines arrived in the Hangar overnight, it was said they were from Sunderland Flying Boats that were being broken up.

The company used to transport three-wheeler foreign cars from the continent into Croydon, they were funny little cars and I believe they could be driven on a motorcycle licence. On other occasions we exported hundreds of day old chicks in boxes to somewhere in the near continent but I cannot remember where. Occasionally these flights were delayed by fog, which meant the aircraft could not take off; consequently the chicks would not survive an overnight stay in the Hangar. Somehow the traders in Surrey Street Market would find out about this and they would arrive at the Hangar having obtained permission to take the chicks. What they did with them is anyone's guess but the chicks disappeared pretty rapidly out of the Hangar.

The Hangar in winter was freezing cold. It had huge doors, which were opened and closed by hand; when this was done someone would shout out "two six on the doors". It took a good half a dozen people to get the doors moving, so different to the modern electric doors whereby you just push a button and the doors open or close as required. As I was saying it was very cold in winter with no heating at all. The spanners you were using almost stuck to your hands, as they were so very cold.

Quite a few people had been to the War Surplus Store near Surrey Street Market, me included, and we bought silk gloves, flying boots and a RAF brown bomber crew-flying suit. These were quilted and had a full-length zip up the front. The only problem was we were not using the suit for the purpose it was designed for. We were outdoors in a cold wind and the suit would inflate and make us look like Michelin men, however, it did help to keep us warm. Old Titch did not bother with any of this stuff he used to come in with layers of brown paper under his clothes and beneath his overalls; he managed to keep himself warm that way. Another huge problem in the winter was the dreaded 'pea soup' fog but more of that later.

Working in gangs of four as we did was very competitive. When an aircraft was due a service check one gang would work on the port engine and the other on the starboard. We would then see who could get the cowlings off first. One of the dirtiest jobs on an engine was removing the oil filter and oil sump plug. Invariably the oil was still hot and as a result hot oil would run down your arm. The biggest task on an engine service check was a compression check. This was achieved by removing the front set of sparking plugs, which was a total of 18 plugs. For this check we used a very high tech tool, namely a CORK on a piece of string! The cork was pushed into the hole or at least part way into the hole where the spark plug had come out, someone else would then swing the propeller as fast as they could, if the cylinder was good the cork would pop out of the hole like a cork out of a bottle of champagne. If the cork came out with a 'phut' the cylinder had failed. This procedure was carried out on all 18 cylinders; you can imagine the noise of one cork coming out yet alone 36 corks coming out of both engines!

The next job on the list to do was the tappets. Both inlet and exhaust values needed to be checked and adjusted as necessary. This was a very important job from an engine performance point. What did happen at times, if you were not very careful, you might accidentally nick the rocker box cover gasket and as a result when the engine was run, oil would come pouring out everywhere. I was at fault one day when it occurred. The Charge-hand was not best pleased with my negligence, I only ever did that once.

One very serious problem we had was the engine fuel inlet manifold pipe. These pipes were about 4" diameter and there was one per cylinder. Fuel would leak from the adaptor, which screwed into the cylinder.

To fix this fault we would remove the pipe and the adaptor and clean it. The adaptor had very fine threads and we used an adhesive, which was new to the market. When it was mixed it turned yellow in colour rather like our modern quick set Araldite. About two minutes was allowed to refit the adaptor and this was achieved with shaky hands and a sweaty brow. We did have a few that set before the adaptor was fully in; this resulted in a cylinder change. A complete service check would take about eight hours. However, if an unexpected cylinder change following a problem was necessary the time could extend by another two or three hours.

Working in the Hangar was great. Lots of banter and a few cross words here and there. The tradesmen worked on a proficiency pay scheme whereby they got an increment of one penny an hour up to a maximum of three pennies per hour. Conversely, if we did anything wrong it could all be taken away again; this misconduct included bad time keeping and too many sickies!

Back in those days we didn't have to worry about political correctness. The majority of people had nicknames and bullying did not exist. But as Boys, we were very aware and cautious of some of the older people who could be a bit hard on us at times but it did absolutely no harm and certainly made us aware of the people around us. From our point of view, being the youngest, we looked up to some members of staff, almost to the point of putting them on a pedestal. In particular we had two lads who were almost 21, Ron Thaxter and Bill Ross that were known as the "Thornton Heath Boys". Bill eventually left the company but Ron went on to be highly regarded and a top engineer and I worked with and for him quite a bit over the years. Incidentally Ron's son Dave set up the British Caledonian website which has worldwide status. He has also written a book on the history of British Caledonian and I am personally indebted to him for his help and encouragement whilst writing this book – thanks Dave.

When I was working in the Engine Bay we had to set up the engine bearer struts. These were the struts that held the engine/power plant in position on the airframe. The whole unit was attached to the airframe by just four bolts. When we were building these bearer struts as an assembly in the

Workshop we set up the height of the struts to within twenty thousandths of an inch to each other. The yokes that held the attachment bolts had to be parallel to within three thousandths of an inch. During the first engine change, which I witnessed, I was surprised to notice the fitters using big screwdrivers and sometimes even crowbars to actually align the boltholes between the airframe and the engine. However, when I started doing this for myself, I realised just why it was done this way. Most of the aircraft had gone through rough times during the war years and some parts were a little distorted to say the least.

Some of the tasks we undertook would not comply with current regulations; it is necessary to remember we were dealing with 100-octane petrol. One such task we carried out was a fuel flow check on a Dakota after the aircraft had undergone a major overhaul. To achieve this test we had to fit an additional fuel pipe to the inlet side of the carburettor teeing it into the existing pipe. The requirement was to measure the fuel flow rate whilst the engine was at take off power. By teeing in at the carburettor inlet we knew we would get an accurate fuel flow recording.

On the ground there was an empty fuel tank on a trailer, a one-gallon container and a couple of clean funnels. The team consisted of two engineers on the ground and one in the cockpit plus an Inspector with his stopwatch. The hosepipe used was about 20 foot long and hung down the side of the engine; the open end of the pipe was put into the fuel tank. We were positioned close to the engine and behind the propeller so we would be subjected to the slipstream from the propeller. On a signal from the Inspector the engine would be started and whilst it was warming up we would make certain there were no fuel leaks and that fuel was flowing satisfactorily into the empty tank. The engine was accelerated to 'take off power' and we would measure how many seconds it took to fill the one gallon container. This check was repeated three or four times to ensure an accurate reading.

Those were the days before earmuffs or any form of safety protection! It was very exciting, very noisy and certainly very draughty. The slipstream at take off power was extremely powerful and we had to hang on to each other to stay upright. It also messed your hair up and took quite a while for your ears to stop making a whistling noise. Ah yes, and the test was carried out almost within touching distance of the 6 inch diameter exhaust tail pipe which occasionally had flames belching out of it. No wonder I now wear hearing aids.

Health & Safety these days comes in for a lot of stick but thinking back to our young days you can see how close we came to having serious accidents. When you also consider engines used to be washed down with a mixture of 100 octane petrol and paraffin in a bucket using a paint brush and polishing cloth to clean and dry it. Another method, which was a lot quicker, was putting the mixture in a bucket and using a stirrup pump to spray the engine down.

When the engine had been removed from the aircraft, the firewall bulkhead part of the aircraft was always covered in engine oil. There were a couple of fitters who had their own method of washing down the bulkhead. This they would do by connecting a fuel feed pipe to the main fuel feed and then ask someone to go up into the cockpit and switch the fuel pumps on. The fitters would then stand with an open-ended pipe spraying the bulkhead with neat 100-octane petrol. These were just a few of the dicey things we did in those days. I am sure there were more but perhaps the horror of them has caused my mind to blank them out.

We did, however, have one incident that could have had serious repercussions. At tea break in the afternoon the engine tradesmen from the Hangar would come in to get their cups of tea. We had long benches about 3 ft high, which were positioned around the power plants for us to work on, but when it was tea break the tradesmen together with their cups of tea would sit down on these benches. One particular afternoon, Wally

Blackman had been removing an aircraft fuel filter and fuel had sprayed onto his overalls. Wally was sitting at tea break in the engine bay between two guys, one of whom had a cigarette but not alight. Wally did not smoke so he was asked would the chap sitting to his right hand side pass him a light. In doing so Wally's overalls burst into flames, he panicked, as you would, and ran to an open doorway. On the way he trampled a wooden toolbox. He managed to get out of the Engine Bay and was running towards the open ground past the Hangar when fortunately an Inspector, Charlie Townsend, rugby tackled him to the floor and put the flames out. If he had not been stopped goodness knows what would have happened to him. Amazingly he escaped with only minor burns.

Another memorable story comes to mind involving myself and two other young lads. We were standing outside the Hangar one morning facing Morton's Hangar when we saw someone pushing a small, yellow Gemini Aircraft out of the hangar and he was doing this on his own. We enthusiastically rushed to help him but on reaching the aircraft he yelled out to us, "leave the aircraft alone, I can manage". We didn't realise it at the time but the person pushing the aircraft turned out to be Douglas Bader the famous Second World War fighter pilot. I believe he was working for Shell Mex at the time.

During 1956 we were hearing rumours about Gatwick Airport being developed and that we would most likely to be moving there in due course. Until then, life went on at Croydon.

We came into work one morning to find a Dakota outside the Hangar with its undercarriage retracted lying on the ground. Apparently it had a mishap on take off and had come to rest at the end of the runway. It was towed from the grass runway to the hangar. The crew consisted only of a Captain and First Officer; because it had been flying freight nobody was hurt. The aircraft sustained only minor damage and was fairly quickly repaired and put back into service.

There was an active cricket team at Croydon and I used to play for the Airline. We used to play lunchtimes and after work using the playing field at Purley Way. We had a very fast bowler, Harry Ayres, who also happened to be one of our paint sprayers. On one occasion I was accidentally hit in the face whilst batting and finished up at Purley Hospital with a split lip, which needed stitches.

Chapter 6

Once I had passed 16 years of age I could do overtime but it was still restricted. I remember leaving work on my bicycle at 17:00 hours, having a bite to eat at home and being picked up by one of the other guys who was also doing overtime. He often offered me a lift on the back of his big motorbike. Another chap had an Austin Racing car he used to race on occasions somewhere near Brighton I believe. He would also give me a lift from time to time. His name was Nigel Lowe, one of our fitters who later became a Flight Engineer, anyhow Nigel one night gave me a lift home and as we were going up Purley Way, pretty fast I must add, my hat I was wearing blew away, Nigel spotted I had lost it, he did an immediate handbrake turn back down the Purley Way, stopped, I picked up my hat and off we went again and by the way it was about 2 o'clock in the morning and no traffic around.

Now it was time for me to get something faster than a bicycle. I looked around with a view to buying a moped; some of them had an engine in the rear wheel. Other options were a Lambretta Scooter but in the end I elected to buy a James moped. It had two panniers at the back, leg shields and a headlamp that used to bounce up and down. It was black and quite heavy, running on a two-stroke mixture, which we used in those days. The fuel and oil were not as clean as they are today consequently approximately every two miles the engine would cut out because the "sparking plug would fur up" so a roadside repair was needed. I had to jump off, remove the spark plug, clean it and refit. Following repair, I would start up and off I would go again. So, between Caterham and Croydon Airport I would break down about, on average, three times and this happened every day come rain, shine and snow. I rode my moped on a provisional licence and when I took my test it was in Redhill, Surrey. The examiner told me to ride around the block and he would watch me at each corner. This meant going around the block a minimum of four times. Yes, you guessed it; the engine cut out and plug had furred up. By the time I had fixed it and got started again the examiner had got fed up and gone back to the Test Centre. When we eventually met up again surprise, surprise he failed me so I never bothered again and just kept riding on my provisional licence.

I was still in the Air Cadets at this time and wondering if I might be called up for National Service. This was something all 18 year old boys were conscripted to for two years. We were told through the grape vine that if, like me you had aircraft engine experience the likelihood would be that you would be called up to join the Army. I was only 16 but this played on my mind quite a bit and I was concerned it might disrupt or even halt my planned career. Very fortunately for me National Service was cancelled 6 months before my 18th Birthday.

By late 1956 I was trusted to do jobs on my own. The jobs I did were checked after I finished them but nevertheless it was a good feeling. By this time I was doing regular overtime, working with Titch and the rest of the gang. I was involved in service checks on aircraft returning from Lourdes making it a 02:00 or 03:00 finish then back into work by 08:00. I was even doing 'ghosters'; it was very tiring and took me a while to get over the tiredness.

An engine change was a real hard slog, especially after working a normal day shift but the money was handy and I had by then bought a reasonable tool kit but as always still needed more. We found that working on Pratt & Whitney engines we had to bend ordinary spanners into weird shapes in order to perform some jobs. This meant buying another spanner to replace the one you had just modified. One of the most expensive tools, which became very popular, was a pump screwdriver. It was about 14" long which when used as a pump action expanded to about 2 ft. The only problem if you missed the screw slot you finished up with a hole in the aircraft. Needless to say these were later banned from use (I have still got mine today) and it still works.

Transair Operations and Engineering Departments were very keen to improve the performance of the DC3 fleet. Among their technical achievements made at Croydon was the design and manufacture of undercarriage doors. When the landing gear was retracted on the DC3 the main wheels were still partially exposed and had gaps around them. Bill Richardson, who at that time was Chief Inspector, designed the doors. Freddie Lord and his colleagues made the first doors out of wood in the Carpenters Shop. The finished product was made in fibreglass and although the main wheel was still exposed, all of the gaps had been filled and this alone reduced drag and thereby increased the aircraft speed.

At the same time as fitting the doors we experimented with a different style of propellers. Hamilton Standard manufactured the propellers. There was a choice of three different types of blades. One was a needle shaped blade where it was quite pointed at the tip. The second was a standard shaped blade, which was basically parallel throughout its length, and the third was called a paddle blade, which became wider at the tip. After a whole series of test flights following the fitting of the different types of propellers, I think we stuck with the standard blade.

Another weight saving measure was to remove the de-icer boots from the wings and tail for the summer months. The airframe lads were not very happy when it came to refit them, as they were a right pain in the backside to refit, especially as you go towards the wing tips where they curved backward.

The engine also came in for attention as some of the aircraft we obtained from the RAF had what was called a 'beetle back' air intake cowling. This was the air intake for the carburettor; it was a very large cowling and quite heavy. It was called a 'beetle back' because it was actually shaped like the back of a beetle. We removed all of these and fitted a much smaller, standard type of air intake.

The paint scheme was minimal with a white upper fuselage, fin and rudder and a dark blue cheat line through the windows. The rest of the aircraft was polished aluminium. Talking of polished metal, we were chosen to do a Royal flight in 1956 to West Africa and spent days polishing the aircraft that was going on the trip. The polishing was carried out by the cleaners plus some fitters and most of the trainees, we used Wadpol to polish the aircraft, it was like wadding impregnated with some polishing agent.

A DAKOTA WITH A DIFFERENCE!

In the Transair Hangar at Croydon in 1956 a series of modifications were carried out on a Dakota, which when completed, made the machine one of the strangest looking craft ever to take to the air. The aircraft belonged to Hunting Geophysics and was registered G-AMYW. It was intended for the aerial prospecting of oil and mineral ores.

Three distinct detector systems, all working simultaneously, were incorporated in the aircraft. The first was a Magnetometer, which measured variations in the earth's magnetic field. Its detector head was carried at the tip of a 12-foot boom projecting from the end of the tail cone. The second system and most sizeable one was the

Electromagnetic Detector, which comprised aerials mounted above the fuselage on struts and a receiving coil contained in a bomb-shaped 'bird'. In flight this was lowered by a winch and towed on the end of a 500-foot cable projecting 200-feet below the aircraft. The aircraft flew at only 400 feet to conduct the survey. The third and smallest system was a Scintillation Counter, which measured radioactivity from mineral deposits. A vital ancillary instrument was a 35mm camera, which recorded the aircrafts precise track. Naturally, the design and fitting of the equipment was not accomplished without difficulty. However, after satisfactory test flying, the aircraft received its Certificate of Airworthiness. The modified Dakota flew for many years but crashed in Saudi in 1967 when it was flying at 400-feet. The right hand engine had developed a bad oil leak so they shut it down and feathered the propeller. The crew put more power onto the left hand engine but for some reason it became uncontrollable so they tried to restart the right hand engine but the propeller would not come out of the feathered position, this then unfortunately resulting in the aircraft hitting some high ground and being destroyed.

On a less technical note, one of the regular manual jobs was lifting the spare set of wings that were in work on the hangar floor. They were supported on three or four trestles and we would have a good 20 or 30 people who on command to lift would manually lift the wing clear of the trestles and turn the wing over. This was usually done on a Friday afternoon, no cranes or mechanical equipment, just manpower.

The access stands we used in the hangar were all manufactured in house by Arthur Soames and one other chap whose name does not come to mind. They were nicknamed the Iron Fighters. Arthur did most of the welding and if we needed an urgent repair to a piece of equipment, out would come Arthur with his welding kit and after a few minutes all would be well. I do not honestly think any of our access equipment would have passed current Health & Safety checks. Our crane used for changing engines was a very simple structure with a handle for winding up the chain. It become a two handed operation when you had the full weight of an engine on the cable. There was a manual brake on the cable drum but it was advisable to keep hold of the winding handle just in case.

Chapter 7

My Dad, after leaving the Army at the end of the War worked in a garage for a while then got a job as a Switchboard Operator at Purley Telephone Exchange and was working permanent nights. Eventually he left the Telephone Exchange and got a job on night shift working for Transair. He worked in the Traffic Department completing load sheets for the night freighter flights. We also delivered newspapers and Royal Mail to the continent.

As 1957 approached the issues around moving to the new Gatwick Airport became more apparent, namely that staff working for the Airlines at Croydon, not only Transair would be entitled to a Council house in either Crawley or Horley upon the Airlines move to Gatwick.

In 1957 I was 17 years of age, I splashed out on a car, and what a car! It was a 1933 Austin 7 which cost me £40. It did well over 60 miles to the gallon and was painted black; well every car was black so it was not unusual in that respect. It had real leather seats but no indicators, all indication were by hand signals. The car had wire wheels and a starting handle that was a permanent fixture. On the steering wheel there was an advance and retard ignition control. This was used to advance or retard the ignition. In order to do this you would move the lever fully retarded to start the engine and this was done to give an easy tick over but producing very little power, this was essential as the car was started on a starter handle and if you advanced the ignition too much you would get 'kick-back' thereby hurting your hand on the starter handle. The ignition was gradually advanced using the steering wheel lever where it was left for the rest of the journey.

1933. Austin Seven Standard Colour Black. I Paid £40 for it and sold it for £10. I saw one for sale at a show a couple of years back for £15,000. Why did I sell it?

To open the car doors on the outside you rotated a normal handle but on the inside each door had a chain. I painted the leather seats each week with a leather paint, which I bought from the local

Ironmongers. Once every couple of months my Dad and I would take the engine out, remove the cylinder head and de-coke it. The engine was a side valve version so we removed the valves and springs and lapped them in with grinding paste.

To lap the values in using grinding paste (a sort of carborundum paste which was very gritty to touch) you would put a small amount of paste on the valve head and some on the 'seat' of the cylinder head, then holding the stem of the value between your hands you would turn the valve stem back and forth until you had a perfect lapped valve and seat (all nice and shiny).

All was completed during Saturday morning and the car would be back on the road by Sunday afternoon. Talking about on the road, although I had "L" plates I was allowed, by Law, to drive the car on my own without a qualified driver at my side. This was due to the Suez Canal crisis on going at that time when petrol was rationed. Let me explain, the theory was that not many people would be on the road. Petrol rationing came into effect in December 1956 and ended in May 1957. The Government issued each person who owned a vehicle with enough coupons to travel 100 miles per month. The coupons were exchanged for petrol at a garage

Petrol cost 4s 6d per gallon, 45p in today's money. Between my moped (doing 60 miles per gallon) and my car I had lots of petrol coupons and could keep both on the road. Believe it or not I actually taught myself to drive travelling back and forth between Caterham and Croydon Airport without the need of a qualified driver by my side.

The low powered Austin 7 really struggled going up hill. For those of you who know the route going from Caterham Valley to Caterham-on-Hill where I lived, the road was very long and steep. My little Austin would go up the hill either in first or second gear. However if I had to stop and do a hill start it was all I could manage to do to stop the car from rolling back down the hill.

At weekends I would be out with my two mates Peter and Tony. Peter was very much into shooting and fishing and Tony was into Jazz and had his own trumpet. He would take the opportunity whilst we were driving around to play Louis Armstrong's "When the Saints ..." Skiffle was the other craze at that time with Lonnie Donegan and we would sing our hearts out with renditions of "My Old Man's a Dustman" or "Rock Island Line".

The car used to behave itself pretty well except when going up a hill. You can ask why and the truth of the matter was I didn't have a radiator cap because the screw threads were messed up so all I had to stop the water coming out of the radiator was a cork which I stuffed in the hole. Of course, when going up hill everything was working harder. The water got very hot and eventually the cork would blow out. Of course I kept a spare supply of corks in the glove box.

The other, not so minor vice with my little car was its cable operated brakes. They had very poor quality brake linings and when driving in the wet they became less efficient. I had to drive with my foot resting on the brake pedal so as to keep the linings as dry as possible otherwise the brakes would not stop the car.

I recall a funny story when I took my driving test for the second time on a very wet day. It was at Redhill when the Examiner said "when I bang my board on the windscreen I expect you to do an emergency stop". So, remembering I had to keep the brakes dry in order to stop; I was driving without him seeing that I was resting my foot on the brake pedal. Consequently when he hit the windscreen with his board I was already on the brake pedal and the car almost stopped dead and as we didn't have seat belts in those days he almost shot out of his seat. After a moment or two when he composed himself he said, "well done very good reactions".

The windscreen wipers were electrically operated and were hinged at the top of the screen via the motor. The wipers were not efficient and didn't work very fast. When it rained hard the wipers would not clear the screen quickly enough. I then had two options, the first was to stop the car until it stopped raining and the second was to operate the little lever in the centre of the electric motor with my left hand whilst driving with my right moving the little lever back and forth. Not the easiest thing to do but it worked. Luckily it didn't happen very often but nevertheless when it did this was a useful trick to know.

I loved that little car, I could maintain everything myself (I wish I had kept it). I look at modern cars today and struggle to locate the sparking plugs let alone anything more ambitious. Whilst on the subject of transport, I learnt to drive our Transair lorry at Croydon. The engine Charge-hand Pete allowed me to drive around the perimeter track with him at lunch times. Looking back at that experience it came in very handy as today, in our family's current life we have horses and most times I drive the Horsebox.

It was during 1957 that houses became available for staff. The majority were allocated to Crawley area and the rest to Horley. We were allocated a house in Horley at The Crescent. From the house we could see the construction work going on at Gatwick Airport. The Crescent and Crescent Way were virtually inhabited by all Airport staff. A funny thing happened soon after we moved into The Crescent. There was a knock at the door and a chap stood in the doorway holding a petition. He was going round to each house asking people to sign in support of his efforts to close Gatwick Airport. Since our homes and livelihood depended upon the very thing he wanted to stop, I don't think he got many signatures.

We had quite a few months travelling between Horley/Crawley and Croydon Airport. It was really quite funny that we arranged between ourselves a system whereby those of us on the same shift i.e. us on day shift would follow each other in convoy fashion then at least we could help each other out with any problems along the way. We only travelled at speeds between 30 and up to a maximum 50 mph for the whole journey; the simple reason was that many of the cars being used on these journeys couldn't go any faster! Mine limited itself to a sedate 40 mph because the hand brake lever would vibrate very badly at anything over 30 mph.

I did mention earlier about the fog, it got known as a pea soup fog. It really was a thick yellowish fog and at times we struggled to find our way out of the Airport onto the Purley Way. When it was very bad the authorities would put out 'goose neck flares' so that from the Hangars you were guided out onto the roadway. On one occasion while driving from Croydon to Horley we were all tootling along in our usual convoy, about 12 cars and as we reached Redhill on the A23 the guy leading the convoy took what he thought was either a short cut or a better route through the fog and we all finished up in a cul-de-sac. All 12 of us struggled to make our way back out and onto the main road. That same night, one of the drivers, Bill Poulter who lived in Chaldon had come off the main A23 and gone up the hill leading to Chaldon, something which he did every day; he completely missed the turning at the top of the hill and finished up in a field. This type of pea soup fog later became known as smog and would last two to three days. Fog or no fog we had to do the journey or lose pay or annual leave, this also applied if you were late. Our maximum annual leave entitlement was only two weeks in those days so any loss was sadly missed.

Chapter 8

By now work was going well and two of us as young lads had been selected to take part in a City & Guilds course. We were enrolled on a Machine Shop Engineering course and this was held at Croydon Polytechnic College. We both really struggled doing this course because there was a lot of hands on working on milling machines, lathes, surface grinders etc. in fact all the machinery that you would find in an engineering factory and we were the only two not doing any work like that in our employment. We attended one day a week and were miles behind the other students who were already employed in engineering manufacturing companies.

I must admit though the theory side of heat treatment and metrology was very helpful later on. It really was the working of the machines that crippled the pair of us. We would be figuring out how to set up the machine whilst the other students were actually cutting and grinding metal. The other lad with me was expelled off the course. I don't know to this day what he did or how he did it but he managed to kill all the power and lights in the College. He was the same lad who tried his hand at boxing and escapology so I guess this was just another experience for him. He subsequently left Transair and the last I heard he had become a Postman.

75

I carried on alone at College but after about a year of not getting very good reports about my practical work I asked the Foreman at Transair, Mr Ankers, if I could come off the course and spend more time studying for my Aircraft Licence, something I wanted to take when I am old enough. He said "if you are serious about a Licence then yes, we will take you off the course", which to my relief is what they did.

The early part of my career when you reached 21 years of age you could sit what was called a 'type rated licence'. You could apply for a licence on any of the following; Airframe, Engine, Instrument, Electrical or Radio. You achieved this by first doing an awful lot of practical work and an even larger amount of theory, both Engineering and Air Legislation.

Once you felt confident to give 'it a go' you had to fill in worksheets and an application form then send them to the Air Registration Board who would then process the paperwork. Once they were happy you would then be given a date for the first part of the process. This process was a multi choice paper with about 100 questions on basic engineering applicable to what you were applying for i.e. if you applied for an engine licence on Rolls Royce Dart all the questions would be applicable to the theory of jet engine and also basic engineering. The rest of the examination consisted of 10 written questions followed by approximately 20 Air Legislation (they were always hard to answer).

This part of the examination took place in Chancery Lane, London, by the Silver Vaults. If you were lucky enough to pass the first stage i.e. the written you were then invited for an interview, which was also in Chancery Lane. You sat in front of two Air Registration Board Surveyors who would then go through your written paper with you answering questions that you maybe got wrong. Once that side was sorted out they would then ask you questions on the relevant engine. A favourite of theirs was to give you a pen and a sheet of paper and ask you to draw the engine from front to back and explaining all the parts as you went along. If and when they were happy with the answers you had given you were then given a grilling on Air Legislation this being Air Navigation Orders and Air Navigation Regulations commonly known as ANOs and ANRs. They would then thank you for attending with the parting words of "we will be in touch".

There were various categories of licence "A" for Airframe Maintenance, a "B" licences for Building Airframes (like we did on the Dakota). Our Chief Inspector, Bill Richardson held a "B" Licence, "C" Licence for Engine Maintenance and a "D" Licence for Engine Overhaul. Instrument, Electrical and Radio were all individual categories but later on they were combined and became a multi "X" Licence. I knew one engineer Hugh Morgan who held a Master Licence; this covered all aircraft up to a certain weight.

Licences were given a unique number; mine which was issued in 1961 was number 10,318. Another chap, Bill Dagnell had a licence number that was in single figures whereas most licences issued in the 1950`s were in the range of 8-9,000s.

The ARB (later the CAA) issued each person with a licence book and every time you sat an examination they were called 'licence on type rating' this was added to your licence book by The Licensing Authority. When sitting additional examinations you would be asked questions on the latest regulations, Air Navigation Orders (ANO's) and Air Navigation Regulations (ANR's).

Chapter 9

I was very fortunate to have got on well with the two main Engine Inspectors, Bill Rowlings and Charlie Townsend, and at every opportunity whenever they were doing engine ground runs, testing the engines, I would be asked if I would like to sit in on the right hand seat and see what was done. That soon developed into being asked to fill in the 'engine run sheets', they would call out the figures and I would write them down. The day eventually came when Charlie asked me if I would like to start an engine, he would start the first one to show me how to do it and I then started the second engine. What a big step this was for me, I really felt special and when I got out of the aircraft I could not stop smiling and I guess I was a bit big headed as well, this didn't last long though and I was soon brought back down to earth by Titch saying "come on you've skived long enough now we have some work to do and that includes you too". He was quite chuffed because he had my best interest at heart in helping me to plan my future.

The Pratt & Whitney 1830 Twin Wasp Engine had a life of 600 hours between overhauls and we had engines that made 600. They would be sent to Field Services for overhaul, rebuild and subsequent return for further service. However, quite a large number never made it due to failure of one thing or another. Most failures were due to metal being found in the engine oil filters. Other failures were caused by bent push rods that would mess up the valves.

The reliability of the piston engine aircraft of the 1950 and 1960 era gave rise to a fair number of engine failures away from base. When this happened it necessitated loading a spare engine on to a freighter aircraft along with a gang of engineers to change the engine.

In order to cater for an unexpected trip abroad all relevant staff needed valid Passports and a full compliment of injections. These included Smallpox, Cholera, Yellow Fever, TAB (Typhoid) and possibly a couple of others depending of the areas being travelled to. The Company paid for these including the Passports. A Doctor at Sloane Square in London carried out the injections. Up to now I was too young to be considered for any trips but I was told when I was a bit older I could go, if selected. They gave me a Passport form and booked an appointment for me to see the London Doctor.

Chapter 10

Modern Airlines have Planning Departments, Technical Records and so on, we, in the 50`s at Croydon, had one chap who did all the Log Book entries. That included engine and airframe; he kept all the flying hours up to date and also confirmed when the service checks were due together with time-expired items. He was a 'real one man band'. Another difference with regard to these days is that wages are paid monthly direct into a Bank. Whereas we had our accountant, Don Lang who, on Friday afternoons would come around to the Hangar with a leather attaché case, place it on the work bench, open it up and call each person out by name and either hand or throw a brown envelope to them containing their wages, we were paid in cash.

As early as 1955 the owner of Transair, Mr G Freeman, had started negotiations with Vickers Armstrong for the purchase of two Viscount 804 aircraft. These two aircraft started operating troop flights in October 1957 between London Airport (Heathrow), Gibraltar, Malta and Libya this was all under a Government contract. We were not to see the Viscounts until we moved to Gatwick.

Transair was founded in 1947 by a handful of friends who since then had seen it grow from nothing to a very successful and highly regarded

Charter Airline. They started off with Avro Anson Aircraft and Airspeed Consuls rose to a fleet of DC3s and now modern Viscounts. Some of the staff that had started in the early days used to tell stories of their experiences. One of them, Pete "Mac" McFarlane, told me of one occasion when they had put one of the Consul aircraft up for scrap but then suddenly due to un-serviceability they dragged it back from the scrap heap and put it back into service. According to Mac the major problem with the aircraft was the brakes; they didn't work very well. He flew with it and when it landed and slowed down he would jump out, grab the tail and bring it to a halt. Of course, this could have been a bit of a tall story but on the other hand, knowing how basic things were in those days, it might have been totally true.

Many odd things happened in those days, old Titch told of days gone by when he was in the Royal Flying Corp and was based in countries of high humidity. They used to strip down the old Rotary Gnome engines and clean everything ready for reassembly. He said that due to the poor properties of the metal used in those days, if you didn't apply oil to all the surfaces, by the morning it would start to rust. Another story told by Charlie Callcott when he was in the RAF in the Second World War and working on Wellington Bombers, one came back from a raid with structural damage. They couldn't find enough material to fix it in their stores so finished up wandering around the Airfield, found some old gas pipe and used that to get it back into operations. Another of Titch's tales was when he was stationed in the Desert with the Biplanes of the First World War. He used to fly in the rear seat and drop bombs over the side by hand. We had such wonderful times listening to all these old stories and I said to myself at the time I am never going to do any reminiscing but here I am, 60 years plus later sitting writing this and doing exactly the same thing!

Now heading towards 1958 and looking back on my experiences to date and mulling over my last three years, I was pleased to have been accepted by the rest of the workforce and also seeing how people reacted to certain situations. One day we had a DC3 in the Hangar and the radio lads released the trailing radio aerial which came out of a tube on the underside of the fuselage. On the end of the cable were lead weights; the lads would pull the cable towards the rear of the aircraft to check its serviceability. On this occasion however they got too close to one of the petrol drain taps that was used to drain off water from the fuel tanks and one was open. Static arced across and caused a flash at the fuel tap and flames started coming out of the fuel tap. Titch averted what could have been a disaster once again by taking his RAF beret off and putting it under the tap, which snuffed out the flames immediately. Never one to make a fuss, he calmly put his beret back on his head and walked off as cool as a cucumber.

A source of real excitement for us boys was being allowed into the Cockpit when aircraft were being towed in or out of the Hangar. The next step for us was being allowed to sit in the right hand seat and put our feet on the rudder pedals to feel how the toe brakes operated (riding the brakes). The day eventually arrived when I was told to 'ride the brakes' and I sat in the left hand seat when someone shouted "brakes off and tail lock out" I would release the brakes and remove the tail wheel lock by operating a little lever under the pedestal that allowed the tail wheel to caster freely in line with the tractor towing the aircraft.

After an engine change or a major service check the aircraft would need a test flight. If it was a passenger aircraft with seats fitted we would be asked if we would like to go up on the air test, of course we all jumped at the chance. If, however, the aircraft was a freighter there were obviously no seats but sometimes we could have a couple put in the back of the aeroplane and if there was enough room they would allow us to fly on that aircraft as well. We had no tickets, all that was necessary was the word from the Captain and off we would go.

We did service checks on a couple of DC3s one of which belonged to Lufthansa the other Derby Aviation.

Refuelling of Dakotas was achieved by leaning a ladder against the leading edge of the wing, dragging a refuelling hose up and over the wing. It was necessary to remove the filler caps and poke a nozzle into the tank. You would then check the fuel contents using a dipstick. This is all rather different from the computerised systems of today.

The Dakota G-ANEG aircraft above was a freighter and was used on long routes; it had a long-range tank, which was positioned inside the cabin.

All of the engine and airframe control systems on a DC3 were cable operated. On a major overhaul the cables and pulleys were removed for inspection. This was a really long-winded process for the Inspectors. There were lots of cables and even more pulley wheels to inspect. Quite a few broken or corroded cables were thrown away. The pulleys had to be inspected for worn bearings. All serviceable cables would then be stretched out between any two fixed points that could be found in the Hangar. We would suspend them about 5ft off the ground and they would be protected with a product called Yellow Chromate. This was a job usually given to the boys, as it was messy. You could either brush the fluid onto the cable that was really messy or use a rag dipped into the Yellow Chromate and rub it along the length of the cable and leave it to dry before they could be refitted.

From time to time engines had to be 'inhibited' if they were going into storage for any period of time. This was achieved by spraying an inhibiting fluid into each cylinder via the sparking plug hole. It was a very sticky substance and smelt quite a bit. When these engines were reinstalled back into an aircraft and subsequently started up for the first time, the whole aircraft would disappear in a cloud of smoke.

One of my last stories about the Croydon Engineers involved a chap called Len Bennett (nickname Lofty), he was a very tall guy and after working a ghoster he was driving home in his three wheeler car when he fell asleep and hit a tree. Len was okay and back at work the next day, minus his car.

Nicknames were so common in those days what with Taff, Paddy, Jock and so on, we often never knew someone's christian name. A good example being Jock the painter, that was all he was ever called in the hangar, it was not until many years later that he married and I found out his wife called him Billy.

In a separate incident that could have been much worse than it actually was happened when one of the engineers was taxiing an aircraft from the Hangar to the Terminal during the evening just as the sun was setting and the sun obscured his vision. As a result he damaged an aircraft parked at the Terminal.

During April 1958 our operation started to move to Gatwick. Some people, including myself, stayed on at Croydon to complete the rebuild of G-AOUD, get it test flown and ready for service. As the Hangar gradually closed down one of our engineers, Alan Jones (Lofty) asked if he could have some of the electrical cable running along the back wall of the Hangar. He was told, "Yes, the power should be off". He got his wire cutters out and the next we heard was a 'bang' and a few 'expletives' from Alan together with the obvious statement to the effect that the power is "not off"! So ended our time at Croydon. It must be a bit confusing reading about Lofty Jones and Lofty Bennett, however, we had a third Lofty join us, he came from a company called Overseas Aviation. His surname was Boake.

I cannot possibly put into words all that Croydon Airport meant to me, as there are already many well-written documents about the Airport itself.

My wife and I visited Croydon Airport in March 2016 to meet with a representative of the Croydon Airport Society. One of the girls on Reception in the Visitors Centre asked if we could book-in and then asked when I was last at Croydon Airport. My reply was, 58 years ago!

Croydon Airport in the 1950s

We were told by the CAS. (Croydon Airport Society) that when the Hangar used by Transair was first commissioned, and before anyone had used it, Lindbergh had flown into Croydon and his aircraft; 'Spirit of St. Louis' had been parked in the Hangar overnight. That is what I call history.

Chapter 11

Before one of life's Chapters ends for me, i.e. the closure of Croydon Airport and another opens; the opening of Gatwick Airport, I thought I would pause for a moment and reflect on just what it was like as a child and growing up during and after the Second World War.

During the first 5 years of my life (1940-1945) I don't remember anything about my father at all because he was away serving in the Army. My Aunt May said he had the occasional few days leave very early on in the War and this was when he was in barracks in the U.K. However, he then went on to serve in Italy and North Africa.

My mother was a nurse and worked full-time, mainly on night shifts. What sticks in my mind about this time was seeing her wearing her starched uniform, a cap with long tails at the back and her cape. Because my parents were away so much, I was virtually brought up by my Nan and Granddad.

Nan would spend all her time in the kitchen cooking etc. I consider that we were luckier than many others at that time in that we had a large garden in which we managed to grow lots of vegetables. Granddad also used to get hold of the odd bit of meat from the Butchers Shop, in addition to which he killed the occasional chicken from our supply at home.

Granddad was quite a 'hard' man but when it came to his chickens he had a heart of gold. I remember seeing him in tears following a fox attack on one of his chicken coops. The fox killed a lot of chickens and just left them on the ground instead of taking them for food. Another demonstration of his compassionate side was when one of our little chicks, only about a week old, had broken its leg. Rather than kill it he made a tiny little wooden splint and tied the damaged leg to it. Do you know that little chick lived to a ripe old age, after such a beginning I don't think Granddad could bear to eat it.

As I said, he was very protective of his chickens because of the amount of eggs they produced. The benefit of having his own chickens was not only for our family; he would give eggs to various people in our street too. However, all changed when The Egg Marketing Board demanded that all eggs must be sent to them. In place of these wonderfully nutritious fresh eggs, we were given dried powdered egg in tins! Not at all what we had been used to but I guess a very necessary change in order to ensure that the whole nation got something to eat. To make the egg powder palatable you would mix in water to produce scrambled egg.

Granddad didn't like my name "Roger" so he always called me "Bob" and did that to his dying day in 1963.

I spent all my happy childhood days with my granddad in the garden and helping him to tend his animals. A wonderful way to watch and learn, so sad many young people don't get that opportunity today.

Granddad and I didn't have raincoats; instead we used large Hessian sacks that were normally used to store potatoes. Granddad would set about modifying the sacks by cutting two holes, one for each arm and a slit in the bottom of the sack for your head. We saw no harm in walking around the garden dressed in potato sacks all day. We still got wet but not quite as much.

At some point after the German Aircraft crashed on the Recreation Ground and Kenley Airfield became a prime target for German Bombers I was evacuated to Wales together with my Nan. We stayed with relatives and we were there for about six months; I don't remember anything at all about that experience, it seems my mind has simply blocked it out.

When the War ended everything was still being rationed. Cars were few and far between and we had a local 'Rag & Bone Man' who, with his horse and cart, would go up and down the road shouting "Rag & Bone, any old Rag & Bone". Horse and cart also delivered coal. Another sign of the times was the sight of an old lady walking up and down our road pushing a pram, no baby in it, just a shovel and a broom which she carefully manipulated to pick up the horse droppings and place them in the pram, no prizes for guessing where they were headed.

Bath time at our house was performed in a tin bath. We had an outside toilet, which stood, next to our coal shed. Toilet paper consisted of yesterdays or even last week's newspaper torn into squares and hung on a rusty old nail on the wall.

Nan's cooking started at Sunday lunchtime and anything leftover became stew on Monday any remnants of which were finished on Tuesday as Bubble & Squeak in a frying pan. Nan was a master when it came to puddings she would make steamed puddings such as Jam Roly Poly or spotted dick, stout stuff to keep the cold out. One of our favourites was bread and dripping.

Perishable things such as milk and butter were hung on bits of string under the floorboards below the staircase in the hall to keep cold, no refrigerators in those days.

Granddad was fiercely fanatical about his football pools and woe betides anyone who made a noise during the radio results. As our house didn't have modern innovations such as wall sockets, the procedure was that Granddad would remove a light bulb from the ceiling and plug the radio into the socket. At once the radio would spring into life and Granddad would settle down to check his football coupons. The results were broadcast on Saturday evenings.

When I first started school each child was given a free bottle of milk a day and the top couple of inches were pure cream. The milk bottle had a cardboard top so that you could make a hole in it for the drinking straw. The teachers at our school were very strict. I particularly remember the metal work teacher having a 12" steel rule that he would smack across our hands if we were considered to be misbehaving. Just to 'ring the changes' so to speak, the woodwork teacher used a piece of wooden dowel, very appropriate I suppose. Whilst the maths teacher seemed to have no qualms at all about pinching what might have been the preferred weapon of the gym teacher in using a size 10 plimsoll (today's equivalent being one of a pair of trainers). He would launch the plimsoll across the classroom towards the offending pupil (an excellent shot, hardly ever missed!) But our biggest fear was being told to stand outside the Headmistresses Office because if she saw you there she would bring a wooden cane down across your hands leaving much tingling to the fingers and a few red marks. I ponder the guaranteed repercussions of such actions happening in today's educational environment.

When I was old enough, on Saturday mornings I would join my Granddad making the Butchers Delivery Round. He had a large meat basket on the front of his bicycle, which he filled to the top with meat. I would cycle behind on my bike. We delivered meat all around Chaldon starting at 08:00 and finishing by mid afternoon.

One lady, Mrs Hall lived in a very large house which stood in its own grounds situated in Chaldon and one Saturday she invited Granddad and me in to see her new television set. I remember it was boat race day and we were allowed in through the Tradesmen's Entrance but were not allowed to sit down. Such observances of rank and status were the norm in those days.

The television set was the first one we had ever seen, it was housed in a huge cabinet measuring about 4ft. long and had two doors at the front. When you opened the doors you could see the screen, which was only about 9 inches square. Such a massive cabinet for such a tiny screen. When switched on everything in the picture was rather green and shaky, it was just about possible to make out the boats on the river, as to who was winning or losing?

Granddad and I did the meat round deliveries every Saturday come rain, shine, hell or high water. However, one particular winter I do remember the depth of snow being as high as the top of the hedges both side of the road and drifting over into the open fields.

I often think of the advances we have seen in the last 60 or so years around the house and things in everyday use. Our Christmas presents as a child I guess in common with many other people of my age group consisted of a couple of oranges and an apple in your Christmas Stocking. Christmas decorations were made from bits of coloured paper glued together to form paper-chains and other such like.

We certainly enjoyed ourselves just as much, if not more than modern day youngsters with all their hi-tech gadgetry and were all the better for it in my view, but I guess I would say that wouldn't I!

That's my personal reminiscence over and back to the main story.

Chapter 12

Before I leave the story of Croydon Airport, I would like to add this write-up produced by Pat Pearce about his time at Croydon. Pat was at the time a student at the Chelsea College for Aeronautical Engineering. Like all students Pat moved around the workshops and hangars, he had a spell at Redhill Aerodrome and in mid 1954 he joined Transair.

This is a direct copy of Pat's story:

"Mid 1954 I started working on real aircraft at Croydon Airport having been affiliated by the college to Transair Ltd. This was great as I had previous memories of the airport. My first visit here was mid 1939 with my father to watch aircraft depart, he realising the war was imminent and the airport might close. Then during the Second World War in one summer school holiday, I watched the airport being bombed from Norwood Hill. After the war when we moved to Purley, I used to watch the rotating beacon at night from my bed and listened to the Dakota mail planes taking off in the early hours. Now I was actually there with larger aircraft to investigate. It was at this time I decided to turn towards electrics which from a boy I had a natural understanding, thus I asked to be attached to the electrical department.

Transair was then operating eight DC3/C47 (Dakota) aircraft, six as 36-seat passenger and two as freighters. Engineering was based in the northern half of Croydon's `B` Hangar, which had the capacity for four DC3's, one of which would have its wings removed for major servicing/rebuild. Around the inside the company had built workshops, offices and stores out of angle iron and hardboard but also occupied a permanent room in the back of the hangar for a sheet metal work and machine shop. The internal buildings contained, apart from admin offices, a canteen, a workshop for power plant build, radio, electrical and instrument shops all of which carried out overhaul work on their respective components. The Company engineer staffing was, I guess, one of the largest on the airport with about fifty in the hangar. There were four of us in the electrical shop and I recall at least six radio engineers apart from all the A&C fitters and several cleaners. Each technical area had an appropriate licensed engineer in charge.

On arrival in the electrical shop I was appointed tea boy as Bryan Tilbury the then junior elevated himself. However, I must say that during the coming months Bryan taught me a lot about the higher power three-phase electrics in the hangar, as his origin was from the Ford factory next door - yes we covered the hangar mains electrics as well as the aircraft. Within a couple of weeks I found I was trusted to do Check A pre-flights on my own. It was great sitting high up in the cockpit powering up the systems and checking lights etc. I soon found myself overhauling generators and starter motors, which was allowed in those days and certified by Bert Parrish our X licence engineer. Three aircraft I specially recall were G-AMPZ the pride of the fleet, beautifully turned out, G-ANEG a freighter with a very large auxiliary fuel tank in the fuselage and G-AMZH a VIP aircraft belonging to a Greek shipping magnet Niarchos, which Transair maintained.

Soon after I arrived Transair brought two more ex RAF aircraft for civil conversion. (G-ANTB & G-ANTC). These arrived from outside storage at RAF Siloth in a poor condition, such that on TB one engine would not stop on its magneto switches and we waited till the fuel in the carburettor ran out with lots of pops and bangs. The first one TB was brought in and completely stripped out with wings off and engines out. I was given the job of stripping out all the RAF surplus equipment, wiring and relays, much of this related to the under belly Para Pack dropping system and remote reading compass system. Then on to rewiring it for passenger cabin lighting, galley, signs, fitting engine fire extinguishing equipment which the RAF did not fit and putting back the original battery system in place of the RAF system. These DC3/C47 were rebuilt for 36 seats with improved performance by reducing the size of the wing fillets and fitting fibre glass undercarriage doors both designed by Bill Richardson the then Chief Inspector.

Some other things that I recall Ground running took place outside the hangar on the sloping grass. One day after a generator balancing run we left the cockpit and on walking down the fuselage found the aircraft was on the move down the slope. The brakes came on suddenly and we all fell to the floor, the engineer had been running it from the right hand seat and having taxied it around then realised that the parking brake could only be applied from the left side. While he climbed over to get to the brake the aircraft ran away. A cleaner, who liked to lean on things, leant on a black pole under an engine only to find the pole was a thick stream of engine oil being drained from the oil tank. Another cleaner who while draining aircraft fuel for cleaning always had a smoke nearby. The front of the hangar had a drainage gully across the doors, which collected anything. One day it produced a wall of flame about two feet high right across, luckily that day we did not have an aircraft parked across it. The day that I was asked to look at an aircraft in the hangar which people said was giving them shocks, I found it parked with its conducting tail wheel directly on a 230v mains lead. A regular trick was played on George, our instrument engineer, when he was sitting high up in the nose working behind the instrument panel. His only access a very tall `A` ladder, which often seemed to move away from the aircraft just out of reach. Security was no problem. One drove through the airport main gate, maybe saw a policeman who did not stop you, parked beside the hangar then through one of the doors to work. No reception or I.D required. The only daunting person was Hank Ankers the Foreman who gave you a rocket if you were late or wasted materials.

Happy days! This part of my life comes to an end here in December 1954 as Her Majesty decided I should join up for National Service, another story another day."

I thought it interesting to add Pat's story as he was at Croydon a year before me and as you have read he found it a full-on job but very enjoyable. He later went on to become an ARB and later CAA Surveyor.

Unlike modern day airlines at Croydon with Transair every component part excepting the Pratt & Whitney Twin Wasp engine and the Stromsburg carburettor were overhauled in house by our own staff and licensed engineers even the propellers were dismantled, inspected and rebuilt. Every metal component part Stringers, Cleats, Frames etc were made in our Detail Shop.

PART 2

Gatwick Airport
1958 – 2005

Chapter 13

Croydon Airport was now part of history as far as Transair was concerned. Our last DC3 Dakmaster G-AOUD, assembled at Croydon, had been successfully test flown and granted a Certificate of Airworthiness from the Air Registration Board. It was flown to Gatwick to join the rest of the fleet, which at this time consisted of 10 DC3 aircraft and 3 Vickers Viscount 804 series aircraft.

All staff were now located at Gatwick Airport and were getting used to their new accommodations.

Gatwick Airport was now our new home but none of us knew at that time what the future would hold for us. There were no whispers or rumours of any likely mergers or expansion plans, these were all kept strictly behind closed doors both at Company Director and Government level (leaks were not common place in those days!) As you read on you will discover how expansion was slow to start with and then rapidly accelerated to form British United Airways.

But April/May 1958 was just the beginning, our first impressions of Gatwick Airport (it was always called Gatwick later it became London Gatwick (LGW)). It was big, it was new, whereas before we had been used to a lot of grass, we now had to get used to a lot of concrete and a lot less grass. The concrete, being new, was absolutely blinding as the sunshine played upon it. As a result many of us were forced to wear sunglasses in an attempt to cut down the reflection and glare from the concrete. Despite the huge expanse of concrete we still managed to park the DC3s on the grass by the side of the perimeter track "old habits".

The Hangar itself, the one and only hangar at that time, was very impressive. It had been built to Transair specification and was designed to house 3 Vickers Viscount aircraft at any one time or a combination of Viscounts and Dakotas. The centre of the hangar was designed so that a Viscount could undergo a major maintenance input without interrupting the other day-to-day operation of the hangar. This was achieved by parking the aircraft 'nose first' into the centre of the hangar, this left the main and nose landing gears sitting astride three platforms which were all connected to hydraulic jacks thus allowing the aircraft to be lowered downward. This enabled work on the aircraft to be done at a much more convenient height and thereby doing away with the need for high lift equipment and scaffolding. This was the theory but I will discuss the practicalities of this arrangement later.

One very striking feature of the 'New Hangar' was the absolute lack of clutter. The offices had been built on the outside of the building and these included workshops and the canteen. Removing these from inside the hangar meant the whole internal area was now available for aircraft and equipment, what an improvement!

Another innovation was the new public address system. Much frustration previously ensued when the bosses were driven to shouting orders at us over the general noise of the hangar. It was only later on that we found we could use the public address system to play a radio through so that on night shifts we used to play music and listen to news broadcasts, this went on for quite a few years, we heard about President Kennedy being shot in 1963 and also some of the American Space Flights in the early 1960s. With the new facilities also came a very efficient heating system, fantastic in the winter, gone were the days of having to warm your tools on a stove before you could use them.

Oh! The new hangar doors, how wonderful they were, electrically controlled, opening and closing at the push of a button, we almost queued up to operate the doors. They were the concertina type doors with each section coupled to the next by a chain. The electrical cable at the top of the doors also moved with the concertina sections. Occasionally we had a problem with the top cable, it would catch and form a big loop of cable, which then hung down, and this could catch the top of a Viscount fin. Everyone in the hangar was very aware that this could happen and when it did, a loud shout would go out to stop the tractor driver before any damage was done.

Above the office block, at the front of the north end of the hangar sat the Managing Director's office. There were windows on three sides, one looking out on the aircraft parked at the terminal, another looking out at the tarmac outside of the hangar with a good view of the runway and the third window looked into the hangar. This third window was glazed with one-way glass so that the Director could see us but we couldn't see him. At this point paranoia set in and a story went around that as he could see what we were doing, the first person to spill oil onto the new concrete floor would be sacked. We were all very careful from then on and happily nobody lost their job.

Initially all the original senior staff remained with Mr Ankers still as Foreman. However, one thing did change in that I could now call him by his nickname "Hank" that's what everyone called him. Over time there were a few significant changes at the top of the tree. Dennis Brookes moved from his position as Chief Engineer to being in charge of all the property. Bill Richardson changed from Chief Inspector and was now Chief Engineer. Arnold Sheead become Chief Inspector and Eddy Dove was now Deputy.

We still kept the same charge-hands though; Peter Peters was in the Engine Bay, with Charlie Callcott and Jack Spain looking after the Airframes. Ted Bath was on Aircraft Engines and John Carroll was on the ramp. There were others whose names, sadly I have forgotten. The list goes on and covers electrical instruments and radio.

By this time we had taken on a few more Engineers some of whom came from the RAF and had jet engine experience. Initially only a few handpicked staff were allowed to work on the new Viscounts whilst the rest of us could only look on with envy.

With regard to the Viscount aircraft, what initially struck us most of all was the different smell. We had to get used to the very definite smell of 'kerosene' as opposed to the more familiar smell of 100-octane fuel previously used. Then there was the oil, by this time the industry was moving away from using mineral oil in preference to synthetic materials, all of which had their own peculiar smell.

Now at the age of 18 years I was still very much involved with the DC3.

I was at home one weekend with my Mum and Dad when there was a knock at the front door. As the door opened I could see our Engine

Charge-hand, Ted Bath standing on the doorstep. He said he had tried other houses but couldn't get any Engineers to respond. He was desperate to get an Engine Fitter to go into work and accompany Bryan Tilbury, our Electrical Inspector to change an engine generator on an aircraft that was stuck in Paris. He said he needed somebody 'NOW' and could I do it? He said he knew I was still very young but he would take all, if any repercussions there might be from above on Monday. So, for now I was first choice and quite possibly the only choice! Ted said he knew I had a valid Passport and felt that I was confident enough to do the job. So no argument, I was to pack a bag while he waited for me and he would take me into work, and so it was.

How exciting! This was to be my first trip abroad. Bryan organised all the spares required for the aircraft, while I just grabbed my toolbox from the hangar and before we knew it we were boarded onto an aircraft parked outside the hangar. Our names were quickly added to the crew manifest (no tickets then to make things legal) and off we all went Bryan, Captain, First Officer and me. What impressed me most and I still remember some of it today, was the fact that Bryan and I stood up front behind the crew all the way from engine start up to landing in France. It was dark when we landed and everywhere was lit up. What a wonderful sight for a youngster, just turned 18 years of age.

As far as I remember, we followed the crew through customs in Paris then went to the unserviceable aircraft and proceeded to work on it. In the meantime, the aircraft we arrived on was being prepared to fly the passengers from the grounded aircraft back to Gatwick Airport.

After a period of time we had managed to change the generator and run the engines, we could now declare the aircraft serviceable. Bryan contacted the crew to find out what they wanted to do about getting back to Gatwick. By this time it was about mid-night so the Captain said "let's get a taxi and go and find somewhere to eat and then we can fly home". Can you imagine my excitement at this, firstly being driven in a big black Citroen taxi, then stopping at a roadside café, ordering strawberries and cream at 2 o'clock in the morning, then being asked by the waiter if I would like Cognac with my coffee! At this point I felt on top of the world.

Back at work not much was said about my late-night excursion, just a few moans and groans but after the dust had settled people were saying to me, "well done". I have to admit it took me a little while to get my feet back on the ground.

Chapter 14

Travel to and from work was a different experience now, gone were the long journeys from Horley to Croydon, instead we found we could actually cross a small stream at the back of our houses, walk through a field to the Airport then use the subway under the A23 by the Terminal Building. You came out of the subway by the perimeter track and walked straight to the hangar passing what used to be the freight sheds.

There was no security whatsoever; in those days you could walk wherever you wanted. How things have changed!

In 1958 Gatwick was a completely different Airport to how it looks today, we only had one terminal building (which is now the South Terminal) it had just one pier (which became the centre pier).

After check in you would go through Passport Control (no security) then walk along the finger (pier) and then down a set of stairs to the gate, you would then walk out to the aircraft. No such thing as moving walkways or air bridges just an awful lot of walking.

The aircraft were parked mainly parallel to the 'finger', they taxied in and out, and there was no need for pushback.

Picture of the original Pier at Gatwick when the airport was opened by the Queen in 1958, picture shows a De Havilland Heron of the Royal Flight and a Vickers Viscount of BEA note the spectators along the top of the Pier (we used to call it a Finger)

It was quite usual at times for passengers to walk out to the wrong aircraft and be quickly diverted back to the correct one, but I do recall that in the 1960s a traffic girl working for BUA (traffic was the name used for the staff responsible for the passengers) stood at the bottom of a set of aircraft steps waiting to board the passengers onto a VC10 flight. We had to point out to her that she was standing at the wrong aircraft and in fact the one she was at had only just arrived. The one she needed to board was parked at the next stand. Well, no one's perfect!

Another function of the 'finger' was to use the top floor (open air) as a spectators' platform. We would often see people on the 'finger' waving to family members as they boarded the aircraft. There was much to be grateful for in old days before security, terrorism and so forth but there you go, 'times change and we must change with them'.

Transair Hangar 1. 1958. Not many cars about. A Dakota parked by the hangar. Not many aircraft down at the terminal. The white buildings on the right were the Freight Sheds. Note the grey perimeter road and outside that the A23 public road.

As mentioned previously, our hangar was the only one in existence at that time and facing out of the hangar there was a large area of concrete upon which to manoeuvre aircraft. Beyond this was a huge bank of soil, which had been laid to grass. The bank was designed and used as a blast bank to run the aircraft engines against. We called it 'Mount Freeman' after our MD. It survived for many years.

When the Airport reopened in 1958 only Transair and British European Airways (BEA) were operating out of it. BEA at that time used DC3 and Viscount aircraft, one of the DC3s spent quite a few days in our hangar undergoing an engine change. BEA engineers at that time took an awful lot longer to change an engine than we did. However, thinking back, I don't think they gave too much priority or urgency to it as unlike us, they had spare aircraft.

Do you know I often think back to those early days and remember the freedoms we enjoyed in terms of there being no security staff; no need for ID passes or hi-viz jackets. Ear muffs (or ear defenders as they are known) had not arrived on the scene yet. In the old days you would sometimes see one or other of our fitters bringing his family around the hangar and showing them what he did. At Christmas time we used to have parties for the children in the hangar, but I will mention a bit more about that later.

We were very conscious for the safety of the aircraft, making sure everything worked and when parts were worn making sure they were replaced. No risks were ever taken, but at the same time we were very careful not to waste money.

An example of this was when one day our Foreman Hank was walking through the hangar and he picked up an 'Adel clip', this was a clip used to secure a pipe to a piece of structure. Hank shouted out "who has thrown this clip away? There is nothing wrong with it, these cost 3 pence each (in old money) and if I find out who it was he is for the high jump". I think this was one of the reasons why, as a small company, we were successful, everyone was 'cost conscious' and 'safety minded', aircraft safety that is, when it came to our own, personal safety, well that was another matter. When I think back to some of the hazardous things we got up to, it was really quite dangerous. But we were young and the Health & Safety at Work Act did not come in until 1974.

Chapter 15

We were all gradually introduced to working on Viscounts but at the same time we still had the DC3s to consider. It was at about this time Transair and Airwork having got together earlier that we found ourselves working on Vickers Viking Aircraft.

My involvement with the Viking Aircraft was quite limited I completed just a few service checks only. The Hercules engines were totally different to anything we had previously experienced in that they had, what was known as, a sleeve valve engine. Also another significant memory of this particular aircraft was as you walked along the central isle of the cabin you had to step over the main wing spar!

By this time I was really enjoying working on the 804 type Viscounts, of which we had three. Namely; G-AOXU, G-AOXV and G-APKG. I must admit to having difficulty in getting used to the smell of the kerosene fuel having previously only known 100 octane petrol smell and of course this was also my first experience of a 'nose wheeled' aircraft with four engines.

Another revelation of the time was the Rolls Royce Dart engine. This was a wonderful power plant with a life span of approximately 1500 hours between overhauls. As engineers we never expected to change these engines for quite some time. And so it would have been but for a couple of occasions when the engine starter motors had been re-engaged before the engine had fully run down and stopped rotating. This caused major damage to the internal engine starter drive shaft; this caused us to make unscheduled engine changes. This crash engagement of the starter motor as it became known was likely to crop up from time to time until a fix was put in place. The fix turned out to be a simple relay that prevented you from re-engaging the starter above a certain RPM.

Another thing we noticed on the Dart was at times you could not rotate the propeller by hand. This seemed to only happen whilst the aircraft was on maintenance. What we found out was that the fuel pump was designed and manufactured to such precise dimensions that the pistons inside the unit would stick to the slipper pads. You overcame the problem by rotating the propeller backwards, problem solved, until next time, when the units were modified it solved the problem permanently.

Other notable differences were the engine cowlings, gone were the days when it took two fitters to remove them. On the Viscount they opened easily by just undoing a couple of fasteners and a few quick release catches. The cowlings opened sideways but stayed attached to the aircraft earning them the name of 'petal cowlings'.

The propeller was another fascinating innovation. Using only your fingertips it was now possible to turn the propeller by hand, a piece of cake when compared to the huge fight we previously went through struggling against the high compression of a piston engine (except for the previous problem we had encountered).

The Rolls Royce Dart engines fitted to our 804 series Viscounts were designated 510 series with a take-off power of 14,700 rpm. Later, more powerful series engines such as the 525 and 530s fitted to the 831 and 833 series Viscounts operated at 15,000 rpm. There were numerous variants of the Viscount usually built to customer specification. For example BEA operated 701 and 812 series, Airwork ordered 831 series and Hunting Clan ordered the 833 series and so on.

We started with the 804 but following various mergers over the next few years we also acquired the 831/833/708 and the 736. Fred Olsen Airline used the 736 at one point and at the back of this aircraft the seats were set out like a big settee. The 708s had been operated by Air Inter (a French Airline) and as we go through this book I will explain the differences between the various aircraft in a little more detail.

A problem we found with the Dart Engine when fitted to Viscounts, H P Herald and Fokker Friendship was that they accumulated air within the fuel system, which caused an airlock. A very important part of our job was to ensure that all engines were fully bled of airlocks on a regular basis. Of course, 'modern day' jet engines don't suffer from this problem.

I recall on one occasion an aircraft suffered an 'engine flameout' while in-flight due to an airlock, fortunately it only affected No 2 engine. The crew had opened the inter engine fuel valve trapping air in the fuel line. In other words, when the valve was opened the airlock prevented fuel from getting through to the engine causing it to starve of fuel. Result, 'flame-out'.

In order to avoid 'flame-outs' Vickers Armstrong, the manufacture of the Viscount, produced a document entitled 'Preliminary Technical Leaflet No 64'. We knew this as the 'PTL64'. It contained extensive new instructions on how to carry out a fuel bleeding procedure. This was strictly adhered to and to my knowledge there were no further fuel airlock problems.

Chapter 16

In the late 1950's (probably 1959) the powers that be required us to move onto some really strange shift patterns. We never did know the reasons for all these shift changes except they tried to match the evolving airline operation.

Firstly, those of us working in the hangar were employed on a 3-shift pattern. These were early shift (06:00 to 14:00), late shift (14:00 to 22:00) and night shift (22:00 to 06:00). The shift pattern was set down in that order, earlies, lates and nights.

One day our foreman, Hank, called us all together and said he had visited London Airport and looked at BEA's shift pattern. He said they did the same type of shift as us but in reverse order. Currently, as I said, we did earlies, lates and nights so night shift finished Saturday morning at 06:00 and your early shift would start at 06:00 on Tuesday. We effectively changed shifts there and then to follow the B.E.A shift patterns of lates, earlies and nights. This new pattern lasted for a while until we went onto a completely different scheme.

The new scheme was to split us into 3-shifts; A, B and C. Shift 'A' would work Monday to Friday (08:00 to 17:00) in addition they would be asked to work overtime on Mondays' and Wednesdays' until 22:00 hrs.

Shift 'B' would work Monday to Friday (08:00 to 17:00) and in addition work overtime on Tuesdays' and Thursdays' until 22:00hrs.

Shift 'C' would work Monday to Friday (08:00 to 17:00) and to do overtime on Fridays' until 22:00hrs in addition to this to work Saturdays' and Sundays' (08:00 to 22:00hrs). Although the new shift pattern was complex we were quite happy working this way. Sadly it lasted only three months as the management began to realise that under this regime we were earning more money than they were! This was particularly so if we consider the weekend working paid at premium rates when most aircraft were flying and we were sitting around doing very little if nothing at all!

After all this messing around we were put back on straight day shifts for a while only doing overtime as and when required.

Looking back on the trials of various working practices it's clear that these were necessary because Airline operation was developing and moving on rapidly week-by-week. Left behind were the old days of a 'Night Freighter Service' and ad hoc 'Charter Flights'. We were now moving very quickly onto 'Inclusive Tours' for

Travel Companies and 'Trooping Flights' for the Ministry Of Defence. We had little or no scheduled services at that time they were the monopoly of the two state Airlines BOAC and BEA. Also at this time various shipping companies were tying to 'get some of the action' by buying into Airlines. However, they soon realised there was not enough money in it for them and quickly withdrew from their holdings in these companies.

Chapter 17

The DC3 kept plodding on with the odd engine change cropping up here and there. A common criticism sometimes levelled at Aircraft Engineers upon returning from a foreign trip servicing aircraft was "Oh you have just been on another jolly". On the contrary however, anyone with a background as an Aircraft Engineer I think will agree with me that 99% of the time on these trips, whether UK based or abroad involved a lot of bl---y hard work, very little sleep and on occasions little food or comfort.

To give some examples; I recall going on two separate occasions to Templehof in Berlin in order to carry out engine changes. This trip was immediately after I had worked for most of the day at Gatwick. We arrived in Germany in the late evening having been flown over on a 'freighter aircraft', not the most warm or comfortable aircraft imaginable. We then had to work through the night so we could leave early the next morning and arrive back at Gatwick. Far from seeing the sights of Berlin all we ever saw was a block of flats by the side of the Airport and the Hangar. A 'Jolly' it was not!

Another engine change to note was one we did in Toulouse, France. Once again we had worked a full day at Gatwick when in the late afternoon we were told 'you are going on a trip' - it was funny how most of these trips happened after a full day's work! Anyway, we arrived at Toulouse airport in heavy rain. The unserviceable aircraft was in a hangar and everywhere was in darkness. We tentatively walked into the hangar in almost total darkness but could just about see that across the centre of the hangar was a wire mesh fence. This, we discovered later was enclosing the other half of the hangar and was being used by the French Military (who were armed!)

Soon after we arrived one of the guards stood at the wire mesh, rattled his gun on it to get our attention, which I can assure you he had without exception! As we were the only people in the hangar (six of us) Jim Marks, who was in charge walked across to the guard with the gun and after a bit of arm waving and gun pointing Jim came back and said "they will keep their eye on us and if we don't do what they say they will shoot". Oh great, here we were in a blacked-out hangar with armed guards watching our every move. We later found out that the guard had told Jim "it is all to do with the Algerian crisis".

We were left with little option but to complete the engine change using torches while the rain continued to hammer down on the hangar roof all night. At around 07:00 hrs a van pulled up outside the hangar and the driver got out saying he would take us to breakfast. Jim led the way getting into the van first, jumping into the left hand seat totally forgetting of course that it was a left hand drive! At last the one little piece of levity in the whole trip. We all had a good laugh and I think it probably served to relieve the tensions of the night. The van driver also recognised Jim's mistake and joined in the fun.

One other, very strange spectacle we noticed was that, strewn outside the hangar were the bodies of hundreds of dead toads – don't ask! To this day I have no idea why, perhaps some French thing I guessed!

We had breakfast and afterwards the aircraft was towed out of the hangar and had all the necessary engine tests carried out. When Jim was happy with the results he signed the paperwork and cleared the aircraft for flight. We refuelled the aircraft and got hold of the crew, having already loaded the unserviceable engine, tools and spares onto the aeroplane ready for our departure. When everyone was ready we boarded the aeroplane and took off heading back to Gatwick. On arrival the aircraft taxied straight to the hangar where we unloaded it and signed out of work. It was now approximately 18:00 hrs. The whole so called 'Jolly' had consisted of approximately 32 hours continuous duty in the cold, wet and dark under the close scrutiny of armed guards and with minimal warmth or sustenance to boot!

After our 'French Excursion', we each went our separate ways back to our respective homes, but this wasn't the end as you might have thought, for we were told at about 20:00 hrs that we had another engine change to do at Hurn Airport, near Bournemouth and further that Hank, our foreman wanted the same gang as for the 'French Job' to do this one as well.

The plan, as outlined to us, was to come back to the hangar at 04:00 hrs, load the serviceable engine onto our flatbed lorry and leave Gatwick by 05:00 hrs. We would then drive to Hurn Airport.

So at 04:00 hrs there was Titch, John Stone, Fred Malthouse, Wally Blackman Jim Marks, Bryan Tilbury and myself. I need to mention at this point that the aircraft was under the control of Airwork Ltd and we were to use their team for any additional help we might need. At 05:00 hrs our driver, Fred Bailey, was all ready for the off and we set out on the 4 hour drive to Hurn.

We arrived at Hurn at about 09:00 hrs and as usual found the aircraft in the hangar. We set about changing the engine, which after some time we successfully completed. As was usual, we ran the engine and cleared the aircraft for flight. This time however, we did manage to get some help loading the spares and old engine onto the aircraft.

Once back at Gatwick, and I hasten to add, back at work the following morning by 08:00 hrs (or you lost pay!) our leader, Jim was called into Hank's office and told to congratulate the lads on a good job! However, the glory was soon squashed when Hank said to Jim "I gave you £10 allowances before you went to Toulouse, where is the change, you couldn't have spent all that?"

Can you imagine how this inquisition might be viewed in light of our modern working environment - having been away for around three days, working for many, many hours continuously with little sleep and all the rest of it? The irony was of course, we hadn't actually spent much of the money at all because most of the time we were eating biscuits found on the aircraft whilst working in Toulouse and we each took our own sandwiches with us to the Hurn job.

Chapter 18

In late 1958 and early 1959 we saw the first new development at Gatwick Airport with the building of the new Morton Air Services hangar and the Overseas Aviation hangar.

Morton Air Services were still operating out of Croydon Airport with the DH Dove's, Herons and Airspeed Consul Aircraft. They ceased operations at Croydon Airport in September 1959 moving into their hangar, which was built on the south side of the Transair hangar. When the day came for the builders to remove the scaffolding and supports from the front of the hangar, which I believe was a Saturday morning, they asked if we could move any aircraft parked close to the hangar and also to keep staff at a distance as, believe it or not, by their own admission, this was the first type of roof and door construction built of this type and they were not certain what, if anything, might happen. You can just image the stories flying around, the hangar might collapse, the doors might fall off, the roof might give way but as it turned out nothing occurred at all, excitement averted! We all walked away disappointed but the builders were happy bunnies.

The next hangar to be built was for a company called Overseas Aviation; this hangar was being built of wood. Overseas Aviation at this time operated Argonaut Aircraft. We arrived one morning to find that a whole fleet of these aircraft had arrived overnight. I can't remember how many, but it was more than six and less than a dozen. Eventually both Overseas Aviation and Morton Air services disappeared from the scene with Morton's becoming part of British United and Overseas went bankrupt I believe. Both hangars played an important part in Gatwick Airport's history for many years, as time goes on, I will explain their subsequent uses and eventual demise.

Chapter 19

Still in the late 1950's everything seemed to be more serious/professional as technology improved, but we still found time for fun and games. One local family springs to mind, that of Jack Register and his wife together with their father Reginald who lived next door to my Mum and Dad in Horley. Reg, the father, lived with his wife around the corner. Jack (the son) and his wife had just decorated their lounge with new wallpaper and they were both very proud of what they had achieved.

There were no mobile phones in those days in order to take photographs and show around in work, so we just had to take their word for the fact that it looked beautiful. A short time later Jack came into work rather upset, and the cause of his upset was that their young son, who was reportedly 'a bit of a handful' had crawled around the lounge floor and skirting boards plucking at any loose ends of wallpaper and ripping them upwards as far as he could reach! The walls now consisted of long strips of bare wall interspersed with smaller strips of beautiful wallpaper! Certainly not funny to Jack and his wife, but it raised a smile from some of us.

Jack was in his early 20s and in some ways 'a man before his time'. He was a very clever lad and he reckoned he was going to design and make a device which would allow him to stand on top of 'Mount Freeman' (the blast bank in front of the hangar) and using his device he would be able to turn the lights on and off in his house. All this just to wind up his wife! Jack and his wife often had rows over some of the clever antics he got up to. He never actually made anything to turn his house lights on or off but it was in his mind. If only he had developed that thought, perhaps the 'Smart Home' would have been invented all those years ago and Jack and his wife would be Millionaires!

However, Jack did build a 'ram jet engine'. This was effectively a tube about 2 feet long with nozzles and an air feed. He brought this apparatus into work one day with the idea of starting it up. He mounted it on a wooden block then; all of a sudden he became over ambitious and connected it to an airline from the hangar. Unconvinced of the possible folly of his actions, he used 100-octane petrol as a fuel! I honestly can't remember all the details but I do remember the thing starting up, the tube becoming red hot, bending and starting to melt – and the very disappointed look on Jack's face, and that was the end of that!

Well I guess all good inventors have to start somewhere!

As many fathers and sons do, Jack and his Dad had the same mannerisms; one noticeable one being walking around with their heads bent downward muttering away to themselves. Jack's Dad, Reg. was an aircraft cleaner and between them they owned an Austin 10 car. One day when it was parked outside the house with the bonnet up, Jack and Reg. were seen walking around it in opposite directions, heads bent and muttering as usual, obviously perplexed by whatever the problem was. Unfortunately, as they were walking in opposite directions, a fact that seemed to have escaped their notice, well yes, you've guessed it a head-on collision ensued resulting in Reg. being knocked to the ground. One could easily consider this to be a regular occurrence as the only response from either of them was their very familiar, funny laughs, which at its height sounded almost like snorting, and this was all that was heard as they sorted themselves out and Reg. got to his feet.

I was with Jack on one occasion when he was about to run the engines on a Dakota freighter version. I should first explain that a Dakota, being a tail wheel aircraft and especially the freighter version, was quite lightweight and if you put too much power on the engines the aircraft could, and often did bounce around. So, once the engines were started you would need to hold the control column back, this would then raise the elevators and so keep the tail wheel firmly on the ground.

To carry out, what was known as a 'ground run', you would hold the control column in the crook of your left arm while operating the throttles with your right hand. At the risk of being a little technical, I would point out that the Dakota had two throttles, which could be moved from idle to take off position. At take-off you would hit a mechanical stop. In order to override this stop and go into emergency power, you had to bend the levers slightly outwards past this stop. The stop was adjustable and adjustment was made by loosening off two sets of screws and sliding the stop forward or rearward as required.

On this particular occasion Jack opened up the throttle to the take-off stop and not being satisfied with the power he had achieved he attempted to slacken the screws. On finding the screw-heads damaged (i.e. he couldn't undo them) he set about filing the stop with a little Swiss file. He then opened up the other engine to take off power in order to compare the two. This meant that both engines were going flat out (something which I had never seen done before by the engineers). Unbeknown to us he had relaxed his grip on the control column, so much so, that the elevators had moved away from their fully up position and were heading in a downward direction. Before we knew what was happening engineers outside the aircraft were fanatically waving their arms about and signalling to us to shut the engines down. The reason for all the frantic gesticulation was that the tail wheel had lifted off the ground and we were almost in flying position outside the hangar!

Jack shut down the engines and rather sheepishly walked out of the aircraft and across the tarmac snorting and laughing as usual. Everyone else was shaking their head and saying word to the effect of "that was close".

Chapter 20

The Viscount fleet were rapidly clocking up hours with regular trooping flights and inclusive tours, which meant we were now getting into major maintenance. A major maintenance visit meant the aircraft would spend four weeks in the hangar. It would be drained of fuel and towed into the centre of the hangar positioning the nose and main wheels over the hydraulic platforms; this allowed us to lower the aircraft. The idea was a very good one but the practicalities left a lot to be desired.

To explain the set up a little, the areas of concrete floor directly in line with each engine of the aircraft had sections into which handles could be fitted. These handles allowed the sections of concrete floor to be lifted out thus forming a neat pit for the propellers to drop into when the aircraft was lowered. This sounds all very well and good unless you found a problem with the propeller or engine whilst the aircraft was in the lowered position. Under these circumstances it was not possible to remove the propeller because there was no room to slide the propeller forward off of the engine prop shaft. This was due to the narrow width of the section of concrete, which had been removed. The obvious solution to this possible problem was for us to remove all four propellers before the aircraft was lowered.

Another problem with 'the pit' was that it was very easy to drop spanners, nuts and bolts down through the gaps around the edge of the platform and when this happened it meant having to climb down to the bottom of the pit to retrieve the bits and pieces you dropped. Further problems arose when using the platforms to work on the aircraft and one was the massive leak from the pipes that fed hydraulic fluid to the jacks, which operated the platform. These problems, one after another meant that we eventually abandoned using the equipment altogether and left the aircraft at normal working height and just climbed in and around it in order to complete repairs.

Major maintenance on the Viscount aircraft was very different from the old Dakotas. Sometimes it was necessary to remove the jet pipe and this involved removing the engine in order to gain access. The outboard jet pipes were easy to remove whereas the inboard ones were a different kettle of fish entirely. Attached to the inboard jet pipes were the cabin heat exchangers and these were held in position on the jet pipe by a whole series of 2BA nuts and bolts (these were the bolts and spanners that had previously fallen down into the pits).

Also during this major maintenance check, the fuel system was taken to pieces. The aircraft had four main fuel tanks fitted in the wings. The tanks consisted of rubber bags, which were accessed through manhole panels under the wing. It was then necessary to crawl into the bags and remove the internal fittings. The bags were held in position by numerous rubber buttons, make no mistake, working inside these tanks was very smelly, claustrophobic and very hot. The only light available was a hand held safety lamp.

Once the rubber bags had been removed from the aircraft we would fit blanking plates to all apertures then pour about a litre or so of kerosene into the bag and seal the last opening. This blanking plate had an air hose adaptor fitted to it, we would then pressurise the bag to about one or two pounds per square inch air pressure (I cannot remember the exact amount). At this point any leaks would be apparent so we would apply French chalk to the outside of the bags to mark the leaks.

Whilst the bag tanks were removed we would take out some of the panels, which were fitted inside the wing in order to expose the engine control rods. The Viscount only had control rods with no cables whatsoever. Refitting the panels was, once again, a game of patience in trying to line up 2BA/4BA screw holes while you lay either on your side or back squeezed into a small space. The lighting, with the bags removed, used 110 volt fluorescent wands, the trouble here being that the wands generated a lot of heat and this combined with working in a confined, very small space, where the only air source was through an under wing elliptical shaped manhole of about 18" x 12" cut out of the wing which was invariably covered by part of your body as you contorted your body to fit and work! Not ideal working conditions to say the least.

When the panels had been refitted the screw heads were covered with tape, now this job would certainly not go down well in our modern working environment - I will explain!

The tape used was called Mylar and the adhesive we painted onto the tape was called Necole. To give an idea, if you were to take the lid off a tin of Evostick adhesive and accidentally inhale it this is what Necole smelt like. The Mylar tape was about 2" wide and you coated the tape with this smelly adhesive then let it set for a while. Then to complete the refit it was back up inside the wing where you would smear some of the adhesive over the screw heads. You would then cut about a 4ft length of tape and clamber back into the wing holding onto the tape, making certain it didn't stick to anything on the way into the wing, as it would instantly adhere to anything in its path. You would then attempt to carefully fit the tape over the screw heads, bearing in mind that the inboard tanks were approximately 10ft long x 3ft high and only 4ft wide – as you can imagine we used up an awful lot of tape, and of course there was no breathing equipment to avoid acrid fumes or protective gloves to cover your hands in case of spilt adhesive which was of an 'instant impact' nature! I can assure you that all in all, it was a nightmare of a job.

The outboard tanks were another ball game altogether they were so small you could not actually clamber into them; only your head and one arm would fit in so everything was done in this contorted fashion.

Having mentioned earlier the use of French chalk it has brought to mind a couple of stories. In the hangar we had two mobile huts made out of wooden battens covered in hardboard and just large enough for 3 staff to fit into. Each hut had a small window in the front as a serving hatch. Obviously they also had a door to get in and a vent in the roof.

The Progress Chasers used these huts. They housed all the parts catalogues and the idea was that we would go to the window, ask for a certain part, one of the Progress Chasers (PC) would look up the part number and write out the requisition for it. The other PC would then go to the Stores to obtain the parts. The thinking behind this system was that it would save Engineers from wasting time going to the Stores and standing in queues waiting for parts. Anyway that was the idea but it didn't work very well.

One of my stories about these little huts was when an engineer took a bag of French chalk he had previously attached to an air supply pipe, up onto the roof dropping it down into the roof vent. At the same time a second guy standing outside the hut shut the door quickly whilst the first one (on the roof) sprayed French chalk through the vent. Result, everyone inside was covered; head to toe in French chalk. Needless to say, those inside were not amused whilst everyone else fell about laughing!

My second recollection on this theme was a story about sticks of white chalk, probably not of the magnitude of my first, but nevertheless worthy of report. Whilst on night shift during a major check on a Viscount, one of the lads, and he will not mind me mentioning his name Harry Leggatt, was completing a very monotonous job inside the cabin and decided to relieve his boredom by drawing little tiny feet going from the cabin up and over the emergency exit and out onto the wing, progressing all the way to the wing tip, finishing with a large 'splat' on the hangar floor and a big "HELP" sign written on the hangar floor. This must have taken him ages to do. Good old days! Nowadays you'd probably be reported, interviewed and most likely suspended for time wasting.

When a major inspection on the Viscount aircraft was completed and everything put back together as it should be, the aircraft would then go for engine testing. This was quite a prolonged business, you had to make sure everything was correct by the maintenance manual charts; this included the exact outside air temperature outside the aircraft. This was achieved by hanging an 'approved' thermometer outside the cockpit window. You also had to take into account the atmospheric pressure of the day and using these two parameters (temperature and pressure), you were then able to work out from the charts what figures you should achieve with the engine being tested at take-off power.

These engine tests, carried out after a major inspection or an engine change were called 'Interconnection Runs' quite a fancy title. It was also known as this for the fact that the engine, fuel and propeller controls were connected together so that by moving the throttle lever the fuel and propeller were controlled at the same time.

Another very important test we used to do in those days and something in my experience faded out somewhere in the mid 1970s was a pressurisation test. This was carried out in order to prove the aircraft's structure. It was necessary to have a medical examination before you were allowed to undertake these checks. The check involved two or maybe three engineers in the aircraft, all doors and windows would be closed and locked. The engines would be started and the pressurisation controls set to ground tests. The engines would pump air into the cabin by a combination of a pressure controller, a discharge valve and a safety valve whereby you had complete control over the pressurisation of the aircraft.

The pressure controller could be set anywhere between 300 and 1500 feet per minute rate of change in cabin pressure and you would pressurise the aircraft up to its maximum differential between the atmospheric pressure outside the cabin to the pressure inside. This, on the Viscount aircraft was 6.5 p.s.i, in other words the cabin was at 6.5 lbs per sq. inch higher than the air pressure outside of the aircraft.

Once you were at max pressure you shut the engines down and timed how long it took to lose all the pressure in the cabin (if you had a big air leak it hurt your ears and sometimes made your nose bleed). At times you could actually create fog in the cabin depending on what the air temperature was around the aircraft. This at times was a bit of fun as one of you could walk down the cabin and disappear from view, another little bit of light entertainment!

Once all the ground tests were completed the aircraft would be positioned back in the hangar and jacked up and an operation would be carried out that we never did on any other type of aircraft, it was called a 'cross function'. It took about two hours to perform and it entailed simulating a flight. You obviously never started the engines but you went through the procedures of checking igniters, engine controls and propeller controls. You would check that the propellers would go into "feathered position". All the navigation lights were switched on, the landing lights were tested, flaps operated and a test done on the autopilot. It was just like going through a flight. After all of this the aircraft would be handed over to the flight crew to carry out an air test.

Something worthy of mention with regard to the Viscount aircraft in particular was that following a major inspection whereby the cabin had been completely stripped out and reassembled, the first passenger flight invariably resulted in the lights and individual air supplies from the overhead passenger service units falling out and being left dangling on the electrical wires and air supply pipes. A bit embarrassing to say the least but they were a devil of a job to fit in the first place.

Chapter 21

Before we leave the 1950s and enter into the rapidly expanding airline of the 1960s I would like to include a little story I had forgotten to mention earlier.

Christmas time on day shift in the hangar was good fun; with any luck we would get away early on Christmas Eve as we didn't fly on Christmas Day and there was a limited service on Boxing Day. All Aircraft would be parked up outside the hangar.

However one particular year was an exception. We had packed away our tool boxes and all was left neat and tidy, just waiting for the word to go home. But instead word filtered down from Hank the Forman, "everyone onto the fuselage and carry on with the repairs". The fuselage section he referred to was a part time job that would, in about a year's time, be built into a complete aircraft and subsequently be registered as G-AHMJ. Apparently someone had upset him so we all had to suffer.

By the end of the 1950s we were operating DC3 and Viscount 804 aircraft. In 1959 however, we saw two Viscounts added to our fleet, namely the 736 series aircraft G-AODG and G-AODH. They had 'done the rounds' so to speak with other operators and prior to our ownership had been with Fred Olsen. These aircraft had Rolls Royce Dart 506 engines and unlike other 700 series aircraft they had rectangular passenger doors rather than the usual oval ones found on most other 700s.

As I mentioned earlier, at the rear of the cabin was a sort of settee arrangement, which we stripped out completely and reassembled to our own standard. Both aircraft were in the hangar for quite some time because we had no immediate use for them. Their arrival simply coincided with the beginning of British United Airways and the fact we were also receiving other aircraft at that time.

I guess over time my memory hasn't managed to retain the exact dates of arrival for each different aircraft and from which company they came. Even my Internet searches seem to throw up conflicting dates, however, suffice to say that from the late 1950s to the early 1960s (possibly taking us up to 1963) we had all sorts of aircraft. A few, but not many engineers arrived along with aircraft and so began the formation of British United Airways.

Before I talk in detail about the various other types of aircraft we had and worked on, I would like to share with you the events of three further trips. Being as I was still, a young trainee/fitter, probably no more than 19/20 years of age, I felt extremely privileged to be sent away on these trips.

The first trip of my trilogy was to Dusseldorf, Germany just after Christmas and into the New Year. A Viscount had overshot the runway, damaged the nose landing gear and bent the propellers. A team of Airframe Fitters went out to Dusseldorf just before Christmas and we, as engine guys, arrived on the day after Boxing Day. In all the repairs took three weeks.

Our makeshift repairs were made simply to enable the aircraft to be flown back to Gatwick and then on to Vickers at Weybridge for permanent repair, which consisted of the following. A fixed undercarriage locked in the down position, a nose section made out of wood, wooden nose landing gear doors. On each engine where the bearer struts attached to the airframe we manufactured four straps as reinforcements secured from the engine struts back to the airframe as we were not certain if any of the engine attachments had been overstretched so these were fitted as a precaution.

My time spent in Dusseldorf was memorable for various reasons but one was the fact of it being the first time I had been away from home over the New Year period.

The Hangar housing the aircraft was massive with a large overhead crane, which was operated by a chap sitting at the controls way up in the rafters. Another facet of the hangar workings was that as hangar staff clocked in for work the data from the clocking-in machine was sent 'electronically' to the Accounts department, quite a cutting edge arrangement bearing in mind that this was in the 1960s and it took years and years for anything like that to appear in our hangars back in the UK.

The hotel we stayed at was about an hour's drive from the Airport and the same German driver picked us up each morning in a transit type van. If he was late due to traffic or weather (it was bitter cold with ice and snow) we would all pile into the vehicle and he would say "Stirling Moss" which meant he would drive fast to catch up the time he had lost and we had to hang on for dear life, no seat belts in those days remember.

On our way into the hangar each day we passed a Security guy who wished us Good Morning. After a while one of our gang said, "he speaks good English, I will ask him where he learned to speak English so well". So one morning Reg, in his best pigeon German, asked the guard how he spoke such good English to which he replied, "I'm English mate"! Just a little embarrassing to say the least.

My second trip from Gatwick was once again in the late afternoon and involved just two of us, Des Symes who was to certify the work and myself. Our task was to repair a Viscount, which had become stranded in Rome due to a leaking fuel tank or 'bag' as we called it.

So Des and I loaded up the DC3 Freighter parked outside the hangar with a replacement 'bag' and all the spares we needed. Remember there were no seats inside a DC3 Freighter at that time. On hearing of our impending trip and not wishing to miss out on an opportunity, Transair Commercial miraculously conjured up from somewhere, an immediate contract to fly out a consignment of newspapers and magazines, this of course resulted in Des and I making the entire flight from Gatwick to Rome perched upon piles of newspapers. I suppose on reflection it was a good way to keep on top of the news!

On arrival we quickly found the afflicted aircraft, which had been parked by Alitalia's maintenance base. We set to work and drained off the fuel then proceeded to replace the bag. It was a very hot and a particularly smelly job and even though, over the years I seem to have lost my sense of smell, I can still somehow imagine that very distinctive smell.

Whilst fitting the new bag into the fuel tank area an Italian guy poked his head up into the hole

147

through which I had been managing to gasp a few breaths of fresh air, basically cutting off my air supply. His motivation was kindness I know in offering me a jug of Red Wine to drink but with my head already swimming with the effects of breathing in aviation fuel combined with having had no sleep, I think red wine was the last thing I wanted to add to this particular combination. We politely thanked him for his consideration and he left the wine for us to drink once the job was done.

Breakfast I remember consisted of a very large plate piled high with spaghetti and cheese accompanied by a bottle of wine. I must say, the engineers out there lived very well in those days. Job completed we flew home with the aircraft.

By this time, and we are still prior to April 1961, we had added the latest Viscount 831 and 833 series aircraft to our fleet.

Forgive me for getting just a little technical for a minute; the earlier Viscounts had micro switches fitted to the undercarriages so that when the aircraft took off certain systems changed over into flight mode and one of these was the propeller control. When the aircraft landed the micro switch (weight switch) would allow the propellers to go into something known as 'ground fine pitch' this allowed for a braking effect. This was a zero pitch but not into reverse pitch.

The latest series 831 and 833 Viscounts did not have a weight micro switch on the landing gear, instead they had a lever in the cockpit, which controlled both the ground fine pitch and the flight mode. The lever was selected forward for flight and rearward on landing. When the aircraft touched down the crew needed to pull back the lever to allow the propellers to go into ground fine pitch. If, however, the crew forgot to move the lever backward on touchdown the likely result would be four overheated engines as the propellers would still be in course pitch position and this together with the throttle levers in ground idle position would mean the engine revolutions were too low for the amount of fuel still being fed to the engine, result elevated engine temperature!

As a side issue here, something both the aircrew and we had to get used to was the different ways of measuring the engine turbine temperatures. On some aircraft you had jet pipe temperature (JPT) this on a 510 Dart engine was a maximum of 670 degrees centigrade before you damaged the turbine. On later models you had exhaust gas temperature (EGT) this was something like 800 degrees centigrade. There was another measure though and this was turbine gas temperature (TGT) and this was somewhere in the region of 1,000 degrees centigrade. It all depended where the thermocouples were fitted, but you really had to have your head screwed on to make sure you had the right temperature for the right engine so that you did not damage the turbines.

Now back to my third trip, which was to Entebbe, Africa. I and three other fitters together with Des Symes and the Rolls Royce rep. Doug Heathcote took the long flight down to Entebbe via refuelling stops in Las Palmas and North Africa. The reason for our trip was that the flight crew of a Viscount in Entebbe reported the possibility of overheated engines, as they had been slow to select ground fine pitch.

John Philips was the Station Engineer in Entebbe at that time. He met us off our flight and took us to his house for an evening and later back to our Hotel. This was my very first trip to Africa and it's funny to remember that despite all the excitement of the flight, landing in a different country with strange surroundings, for me the technical side of why we were there took preference over all else.

We had a night's sleep and the next morning at the Airport we removed some of the combustion chambers from the Viscount's engines to inspect the turbine sections. The inspection of the turbines was carried out in those days by the use of a torch and good eyesight; we had none of the modern technology just good old number one eyeball technology. We actually found no damage at all, so simply reassembled everything, carried out some engine runs and declared the aircraft serviceable and flew back home on it this time stopping off in Khartoum.

We had much more freedom in those days, it was possible to stand behind the crew and watch what was going on. I remember the landing in Khartoum, it was very hot on the approach and the Captain said he was having a little difficulty in getting the aircraft down onto the ground because of the effect of the heat! Quite how much of this was truth and how much was just him trying to impress me I will never know!

The working atmosphere was very much more relaxed between flight and cabin crews in those days; we had one particular Captain and First Officer who loved winding up new and inexperienced cabin stewardesses. I remember on one occasion the Captain asked one of the senior girls to bring him up a tin of tomato soup, then both the Captain and First Officer proceeded to pour said soup into their sick bags. After a short while they invited the young stewardess, who was on her first trip, to come up to the flight deck. On arrival she saw both the Captain and First Officer spooning soup out of their sick bag and eating it. As you can imagine, she turned a

151

bit green around the gills but she learnt her job pretty quickly after that.

One memorable aircraft belonged to Airwork, which was the 831 series Viscount. It was leased to Sudan Airways and we maintained it at Gatwick. It was absolutely beautiful, painted in Day-Glo colour paint (what we would call fluorescent paint these days). It was painted Blue and Yellow and called the 'Blue Nile Viscount' registered as ST-AAN. The blue paint represented the Blue Nile River and the yellow represented the Desert. It flew between London, Cairo, Beirut and Khartoum back to Cairo and onto London.

Sudan Airways Viscount 831 Series Beautiful colour scheme

152

Chapter 22

1961 heralded a new direction for me; I finished being classed as either a trainee or improver. We tried to become reclassified as apprentices but Government rules would not allow it. So that's that, I am now a fully trained 'Engine Fitter' with 5 years training under my belt having been trained by some of the most skilled and pedantic fitters you could ever wish to meet and I am extremely grateful to all of them.

Viscount 804 Series at Gatwick in Hangar 1 late 1950s the 2 people in suits are on the left Bill Richardson Chief Inspector and on the right Captain Stan Webster, Transair Chief Pilot. You can just make out the pit covers on the hangar floor and also a row of DC3 Propellers.

Some of the lads in Hangar 1 at Gatwick early 1960s on the steps with red collar is Ron Archer next to him is me, the tall guy with the white hat was lofty Boake -you did not mess with him.

At this point I decided to apply for a Maintenance Engineers Licence at the very first opportunity and that would be on 25 April 1961, my 21st birthday.

My first step was to find out what I needed to study and what from a practical point of view was needed. I made up my mind to apply for a 'Type Rated Licence' on the Rolls Royce Dart 510 engines. In order to make my application I needed to fill in work experience sheets, this was not difficult because by now there was not much on a Dart engine that I had not taken apart or repaired.

To continue I needed to master Jet engine theory and this involved various recognised laws such as Newton's Third Law of Motion, Charles Law on temperature and pressure and so on. I will not go into detail regarding these Laws because anyone not involved with Jet engines will probably be bored to tears and those who have worked on Jet engines will know all about this anyway.

So let's press on with some of the other subjects I had to learn, namely basic engineering. As you can imagine this is a vast subject and basically it was a matter of potluck as to whether I had covered enough of the information in order to pass the exam. To give a rough idea, the questions ranged from "how would you check bearer strut for a bow"? "How do you wire lock a nut and bolt correctly" (i.e. how many twists of the wire must there be to an inch)? It sounds rather pedantic doesn't it, but that is precisely how accurate every single operation needed to be in order to pass.

The next phase of learning (the subject feared most of all) came in the form of "Legality". In order to read up on this I needed to purchase from Her Majesty's Stationery Office three copies of official regulations as follows: Air Navigation Orders, Air Regulations and British

Civil Aircraft Regulations Section L (BCARs) which dealt with Aviation Licensing. If I am totally honest, I started reading these legal documents during the spring of 1961, I would sit in the garden either before or after my shift started or finished and just read, trying to take everything in. I spent days and days reading without understanding a word of it but the hope was that somewhere, somehow something would stick and re-emerge just when I needed it most, ever the optimist! I would read 20 or so pages and none of it seemed to sink into my brain. Then, one afternoon I experienced one of those special moments in life when everything starts to make sense, not sure to this day what the trigger was but after that I gradually managed to get the hang of it all.

The Company, realising I was serious in my attempts to obtain my licence, sent me on a Rolls Royce, Manufacturers Course for Dart Engines. The course lasted two weeks and was based in Derby so my career path seemed to be establishing itself and I was quietly delighted with what I had achieved so far.

Chapter 23

If we flip back a couple or so years in my story I sold my faithful old Austin 7 car for £10, a lot of money in those days, and bought a 1946 (or was it 1948, I can't quite remember exactly) Ford Popular and yes it was Black, Henry Ford's most famously quoted favourite colour! It was an 'all right' sort of a car but after a while the boot at the back of the car started to rust badly. There was a door, which dropped downward to expose the boot area, and it was this door that started to rust so badly. As my Dad was quite handy at repairs he filled the whole of the lower part of the door with filler and when it was rubbed down and painted honestly, you couldn't see where the repair had been made. With hindsight, what a clever man he was in being able to turn his hand to most things, well you had to in those days, no 'While U Wait Body Repairs' available, most things were DIY.

When eventually, sometime in 1960, we took the car to a garage in Purley, Surrey in order to part exchange it for another car, the salesman looked around it and said "nice car, really good repair to the boot". We asked how he could tell it had been repaired and he said "all Ford Popular cars of that age rusted out at the bottom of the boot door". Anyhow we exchanged it for a two-year-old Vauxhall Cresta, 1958 model. The Vauxhall had a two-tone paint scheme, Silver and Blue.

157

Bought brand new it cost somewhere around £600 but I bought it for £400. It had a 2-litre petrol engine and a 3-speed gearbox. The gear change was on the left-hand side of the steering wheel, latterly known as a 'column change' vehicle. The gearbox on this car was extremely forgiving in as much as it would allow the car to pull away merrily in top gear, so to some extent this was all you really needed.

Another refinement of this car was its 'all leather interior' and comprised a bench seat at the front and another bench seat at the rear but this one had arm rests in middle of the seats. All of the attachments were chrome, bumpers, wheels, door handles and even the complete dashboard was chrome. Of course the biggest downside to all this beautiful chromed effect was corrosion! A further innovation for the time was the 'automatic choke' but I'm not sure that the technology was quite there at the time because it would either stick open or closed and was quite difficult to get at it.

Fast forward again to February 1961 and off I go to Derby for my Dart engine-training course.

I travelled alone to Derby in my Vauxhall Cresta arriving at my company sponsored B&B lodgings that were quite near to the factory where my training was to take place. On arrival I found I was sharing a room with another Engineer called

Dave Record. He had previously been working in Germany and was booked on the same course as me. We hadn't met before but he seemed pleasant enough and our paths crossed many times over the years.

The course was enjoyable and I learnt a lot. On the drive home however, I noticed that the clutch was playing up, not allowing me to select the gears properly or cleanly so there was no option for me but to stay in top gear all the way home. Thank goodness for that 'all forgiving gearbox' I knew it would come into its own one day and what a powerful car that was!

Chapter 24

The scene was now set for my attempt at attaining my Licence. Our Chief Inspector countersigned all my completed paperwork and I sent it off to the Air Registration Board. Now the waiting to hear of an exam date began.

Eventually I was given a date for the exam to be held at Chancery Lane, London. I sat the exam a couple of days after my 21st birthday. Having not travelled to Chancery Lane before, being a 'country boy' so to speak, I found it quite a challenging place to get to. Now I had to wait for about two weeks for my results, I then received a letter informing me I had failed the examination. Rather unhelpfully the letter didn't say whether I had failed the multi choice or the written questions, so it was simply a case of back to the books and try again with a lot more studying. Old Titch who you may remember I worked with, had a good philosophy he said "if I had passed first time you would only have learnt what you had studied, but being forced to read more you now have a much greater knowledge". I am not so sure he was right but that was his belief and I would not argue with him.

As previously mentioned, the late 50s and early 60s saw many different Airlines and aircraft operating out of Gatwick Airport.

It was one dark, miserable, wet night that I along with the rest of our gang were working night-shift and were asked to go down the ramp (this was the name we used for aircraft at the Terminal), as an American aircraft needed engine assistance.

On arrival we discovered the aircraft was a Lockheed Constellation, Model 0749. The initial problem seemed to be that number four engine (starboard outer engine) had lost a lot of oil. Upon inspection we found the sump plug was loose in its fitting and it was relatively simple to tighten the sump plug and refill the oil tank, job done. However, on further investigation we found that number three engine (starboard inner) had an electrical generator failure, it transpired that this was due to a drive shaft failure, in fact it had completely sheered in half. Unfortunately we didn't have spares for this particular failure so we had no other option but to replace the original generator and leave it unserviceable.

Sadly the problems didn't end there as number two engine (port inner) registered a fluctuating cylinder head temperature, which we found was due to the thermocouple that is fitted between the cylinder head and the sparking plug working loose. Hurrah! Number 1 engine (port outer) was operating correctly.

Following the repairs, as we attempted to replace the cowlings on number two engine, we found they were extremely difficult to fit in fact it was necessary to employ the services of one very large hide-faced hammer together with a comparable sized screwdriver to effect the refit! The most surprising thing of all for us was that when we turned around and looked towards the cabin of the aircraft we saw all the passengers peering at us out of the windows! We hadn't realised they were still on board.

In those days you could float between work in the hangar or on the front line, to help out. Neither did we have fixed contracts between the Airlines, so if somebody wanted assistance it was just a matter of signing a piece of paper in the Engineering Office and the job would be done and somehow our Airline would eventually get paid.

However, there was one slight hiccup in this otherwise flexible arrangement and that was when I was sent to refuel a Viscount Aircraft. Unfortunately, I mistakenly refuelled the wrong Aircraft. Luckily for me the fall-out from this situation was deftly contained within our Engineering Office and sorted out with the Captain of the aircraft, who, as you can imagine, was entirely happy as it saved him getting wet, he simply signed the paperwork and we eventually got paid.

Chapter 25

Some months passed and I was by this time well into my studies again and I reapplied to the Air Registration Board to retake my examination. It was very helpful for me that on this occasion two of the older engineers in the hangar (Robbie Warren and Ron Frampton) were also aiming to sit the same examination, so we were able to bounce questions off each other to the benefit of us all.

So again I travelled to Chancery Lane, London, where I re-sat the basic examination, 3 months after my 21st birthday. I felt much more confident this time than the first but I still had the agonising wait for confirmation of pass or failure. This time when the letter arrived I was delighted to see that I had passed and was invited back to London for an interview. I must admit to having been quite nervous, this was the first time I had sat across a table being quizzed by two Air Registration Board Surveyors.

The dreaded interview took the rough format as follows: The interviewers firstly went through my written papers and asked me extra questions regarding the ones I had answered incorrectly. One I remember very well, it was a question about how you check the bow on an engine bearer strut to which I had answered, "Well you use a Three Point Trammel". I had read this somewhere during the course of my 'reading-up' prior to the examination, however, in real life, we never used one, we always used a couple of 'V' blocks on a surface table, with a Dial Test Indicator (DTI) or a straight edge with feeler gauges. So when they asked me how to use this 'Trammel', I was really not certain at all how the thing worked. The examiner obviously guessed I was struggling to explain myself then he started to ask me as to which of the Three Points of the Trammel was adjustable. Well by this time I must have looked absolutely blank and finally I stopped digging that particular hole and just said, "I must admit, I have never used one. ... or indeed ever seen one". He said, "Right let's start again, what do you use to check the bow?" Seeing that further bluff was totally futile I simply told him the methods that we used, at this point he raised his hands into the air and said, "why didn't you say that in the first place?" Just to hammer home the point he then told me "no one uses a Trammel these days". After that he seemed quite happy that we had got to the bottom of the issue and we pressed on talking about the Dart engine and what series of engines I had worked on, phew!!!

The interview lasted approximately 2 hours when finally they asked me some Air Legislation questions after which they thanked me and said they would be in touch.

So it was back to working shifts in the hangar after the interviews, Robbie, Ron and I were all in the same boat, just waiting to hear how we had all got on.

Finally the long awaited news came when I had been working on an early shift in the hangar, finishing at 14:00 hrs, after which I went home. My Mum had left me some lunch that I just needed to heat through, but before I could get to it, there came a knock at the front door. When I opened it there stood Eddie Dove, (who was now our Deputy Chief Inspector). At the very sight of him standing there my poor little heart started beating 90 to the dozen and my brain was besieged with dire thoughts of just what I could have done wrong that would carry such serious implications to bring HIM here!

He looked at me and said, "We have just telephoned the ARB about your exam... I am pleased to tell you that you are now a qualified, Licensed Aircraft Engineer, Congratulations". With very little time for me to fully absorb his delightful news, he then said, "now, how would you like to become an Inspector"? To which I, still flushed with success, energetically replied "YES PLEASE"! A long held dream seemed fulfilled and so it was agreed. He said, "Okay, then put your coat on and come with me straight back to work and join the afternoon shift as an

Inspector". At this point total excitement took me over and lunch was completely forgotten.

Some, time later Eddie told me that I was at that time the youngest person to have achieved these qualifications. I'm glad to say that the news was also good for Robbie and Ron too both of whom passed their exams.

So this was my first step upon the promotional ladder at the tender age of just 21 years. Rather different from today's methods of promotion. I didn't have a CV, nor did I apply for the job and there was no interview. They simply asked if I wanted the job of Inspector and once I agreed I was just told to get on with it. There was no 'on the job training' nor was there any kind of induction course. Oh! I'm not forgetting Health and Safety Law here either; there wasn't any it hadn't been invented yet! Happy Days.

On my arrival back at work, I was told to go to stores, hand in my white boiler suits and exchange them for three white coats. I also collected a regulation torch and mirror together with an Inspection Stamp and new inkpad. One other essential piece of kit in my new role was an A4 size clipboard to hold my inspection sheets.

Now fully equipped and ready to go, my first job as an Inspector was to do a complete inspection of the aircraft that I had been working on as a fitter a few hours earlier in the day. How bizarre was that!

The three shifts of Inspectors each had a compliment of 2 Airframe, 1 Engine, 1 Electrical, 1 Radio and 1 Instrument Inspectors. The leader of the shift was called a 'Section Inspector' who basically looked after us all and allocated us to various aircraft. Worthy of note is the fact that I only ever refer to 'he' or 'him' in this text and there is good reason for it, since at this time, in Engineering there were only a couple of female staff whose responsibilities were entirely administration based. There were no female members of staff working on aircraft at this time.

I must say the change in my duties felt very strange, all that was required from me was to initially raise defects found on the aircraft; write them on an Inspection Sheet and hang the sheets on the Inspection Board adjacent to the aircraft. We then went back to the office and waited until it was time to inspect the finished work. This was the theory anyway, but invariably we went back out to the aircraft and engaged with the fitters giving guidance as to how to fix the problems. There were strict dividing lines between 'Inspection' and 'Production' staff. On occasions we would find that the Production Chargehand would try to get some of the panels refitted to the aircraft before the Inspector had given clearance. One of our Chargehands had a theory that if you refitted 20 or so panels and the Inspector said remove 10 of them so I can complete my inspection, the Chargehand reckoned he was ahead of the game in trying to get the aircraft completed. I must admit he had a point because along the way I had come across Engineers promoted to Inspectors who seemed to have thought that the aircraft had been in the hangar for their benefit so that they could learn more about the aeroplane to the point where they had lost sight of the fact that the aircraft was needed as soon as possible back into service.

Chapter 26

After a few months spent in the hangar on Inspection duties, on one particular day I was called into Eddie Dove's office. He told me that the Outstation Manager, Jim Smith would like me to take some trips abroad for him.

To explain Jim's role, I need to tell you that Gatwick was known as 'Our Main Base', the hangars were called the 'Maintenance Base', and the terminal area was known as the 'Main Station' more commonly known to us as 'the ramp'. In those days Engineers were based in some of the more remote places i.e. Entebbe, Cairo, Khartoum, Las Palmas and a few others. These were known as 'Outstation Engineers' and they were directly responsible to Jim Smith. He also had responsibility for other operations that were not of a local nature and on occasion he would need an Engineer to fly with the aircraft in order to fix any problems and undertake refuelling etc. Our name for these people was 'Flying Spanners' and this was what Jim wanted me to do for him.

This was quite something for me bearing in mind I am still only 21 years old here and I've only been qualified for a short time. The fact that the Engineering Management had confidence enough in me to do the job, I felt, was quite remarkable.

I was told to go to Uniform Section and pick up a uniform and then report to our new promoted Chief Inspector, Arnold Sheead (Bill Richardson who was previously Chief Inspector is now the Chief Engineer and Dennis Brooks has now been put in charge of Works & Bricks & Property), in order to receive my instructions. I duly got my uniform (second hand) and reported to Arnold. His words went something like this "right, we know you can do the job and your existing Engineering Approval has been extended to cover the whole aircraft, in other words you have approval to fix any problem that might occur and the only time we want to hear from you is if the aircraft has been damaged to such an extent that you cannot repair it yourself". WOW! That made my head spin rather I can tell you. So where did they send me on my first trip, all the way down to Accra, West Africa - a whole week away on my own!

This flight to West Africa was a route that Hunting Clan Airline used to operate and was called a Coach Service Route. We, BUA, operated the route with 833 series aircraft (Viscounts), formerly in the Hunting fleet.

The trip was routed via Lisbon and then onto Las Palmas where we night stopped. We then went on down across North Africa where I think we refuelled in Benina then down to Bathurst and finally across to Accra. The same crew operated it there and back.

An engineer, Jim McClean who had done this trip a few weeks previously, had warned me (I had a lot of respect for Jim). He said "when you are in Bathurst be careful if you have to change a wheel, the jack you use to raise the aircraft will probably sink into the soft surface because during the War everywhere was covered in the old metal strips used on Air Force Stations". He said "take a piece of wood with you to spread the load under the bottle jack that you use to jack the aircraft with". A main wheel change was a bit of a nightmare anyway because to save weight on the aircraft we only carried a spare tyre not a wheel assembly. All I can say is, I was very thankful we didn't need to replace anything. However, my only problem was filling the domestic water supply because they didn't have the correct fitting so I had to fill the tank by climbing up into the aft freight hold and filling the tank through an access panel. It was late morning and very, very hot. I came out from the freight hold dripping wet with sweat and then had to get on with the refuelling.

The Viscount had electric starter motors for the engine and you therefore used an external power source for engine starting. This unit was called a Houchin and was an engine driven unit that supplied electrical power. However, when we arrived at the site we found the rig was unserviceable and there was no other means of external engine starting. Bearing in mind it was extremely hot outside we had to resort to doing an internal battery start. Under normal circumstances it would not be our option of choice as it was a huge drain on the aircraft batteries, however, considering the very hot conditions we just kept our fingers crossed hoping we could start the engines. Our plan was to start one engine then open the throttle on that engine this would enable the engine generator to come on line and we could then start the other three engines.

We were able to overcome some of the problems regarding the heat with the Viscount/Dart combination by 'milking the fuel valve'. This was achieved by slowly opening the high-pressure fuel valve in the cockpit as the engine spooled-up, you could then control the engine temperature and avoid overheating.

We then arrived in Accra; I stayed with the aircraft to get it ready for the next day whilst the crew went off to the hotel. Once the aircraft was serviceable, I made my way to the hotel. What I remember most was having a bath, there was no shower, and even worse there was no air conditioning in the hotel.

We had arranged to have dinner that evening together so I changed into my green suit, put on my cravat, we wore those at times instead of a tie, and these were very trendy for young males in those days! I also wore my 'winkle picker' shoes. For those who don't know what they are, well they were normal shoes with long pointed toes that tended to curl up at the end. Despite the bath and change of clothes and due to the lack of air conditioning, I was as hot as I had been all day, then we sat down at the table and ate chicken curry, what an experience!

Our trip back to Gatwick went without a hitch and I was back in the hangar working the following day.

A few weeks later I was called upon again this time to go to Cyprus, that had its own memories mainly due to the fact that the aircraft door seals had lost air pressure, therefore there was a continual loud whistling noise coming from the passenger doors during flight. Once we were on the ground, I tried to find some air charging bottles so that I could top up the air pressure in the supply bottle, which on the Viscount was located in the nose landing gear bay. However, I couldn't find any on the civil side of the airfield and as where we had landed was also an RAF Station; I found a sergeant and asked him if he could help. He called an airman over and said to him, "help this officer, and get him what he wants". I was so chuffed to have been mistaken for an officer, it really made my day.

A few months later I went to an Island quite close to Madeira called Porta Santa. We flew out empty from Gatwick, the idea being to bring back an aircraft load of package tour holidaymakers.

The runway was virtually the whole length of the Island and it had just one hotel by the beach. My lasting memory was that the hotel had about 100 rooms, all of them empty! The Island seemed so deserted that I took some cine film on the beach and my footsteps were the only ones to be found. I wonder what it looks like today?

Before we left Gatwick, I asked Jim (the boss) what the procedure for refuelling was on the Island. He said "no idea, we have never been there before, sort it out when you get there". When we landed on the Island our radio set was playing up and I had to sort it out. The Authorities came over to us at the aircraft, took our Passports together with the Aircraft Log Book, saying we would get them back when we left.

The passengers arrived the following day on a Ferry Boat from Madeira. I always remember the Captain, Bill Cumbus, had a lucky mascot that he hung from the front windscreen sun visors. The mascot was called Lolita

I did not do any more trips for a while, we had a lot of work on in the hangar, by this time we had Hunting Clan and Aviation Traders Bristol Britannia's, a really advanced aircraft for its time with lots of electrics, even the throttle and fuel cocks were electrically controlled.

We used to work on these aircraft outside in the open because the hangar we had wasn't large enough to accommodate the whole aircraft. Hank, our Foreman, gave the problem quite a bit of thought and eventually came up with a system, which resembled a railway track. The idea was that we would be able to push the aircraft into the hangar sideways. However, this method was employed just once when on the inaugural test-run we found only one wing and two engines would fit in at a time. So we abandoned the experiment completely and simply carried on working outside which wasn't too much of a problem except when it came to completing a full service check taking the best part of 3 days. Under these circumstances we were at the mercy of the good old British weather conditions, which were not always in our favour. If we happened to get caught mid-service as it began to rain, all external panels had to be refitted immediately and engine cowlings needed to be closed as you can imagine this added considerably to the service time allowed. Each service check engine run took approximately 1½ hours to complete.

Chapter 27

In the very early days of British United Airways the Company decided it was time for a new look Livery Scheme and so an internal competition was held to see who could come up with the best design for a tail fin, something to really make it stand out from the crowd. The eventual competition winner had designed something resembling a red lollypop, which was cautiously received by the Company. So before rushing ahead to re-spray the entire fleet the company gave authorisation for just one Viscount tail fin to be painted. In hindsight this was a very smart move since the ultimate consensus of opinion was that the new livery was a huge flop, which didn't go down at all well. Needless to say, the new livery was quickly scrapped and the whole idea was brushed under the carpet and soon forgotten.

By this time (1961/62) we had a real mixed bag of aircraft to work on. At one point they even flew in a helicopter with the express purpose that we should work on it. My lasting impression of this quirky deviation from the norm was that as the paint was stripped off from the helicopter's structural metal it was found to be so heavily corroded that nothing could be done to save it. Eventually defeat was conceded and it was taken away on a flatbed lorry for scrap. Here ends my experience of working on helicopters, shame really it would have been another string to my bow.

I was asked to work on a Vickers Valleta aircraft belonging to the Decca Navigation Unit, which I found parked outside our hangar. On entering the cockpit in order to make a start I, being of the slightly taller persuasion, would inevitably crack the top of my head on a 'box of tricks' hanging down from the roof. It subsequently transpired that this boxed unit contained all the necessary 'mumbo-jumbo' considered necessary for mapping. It's true to say I remember this job well!

Another aircraft we worked on was a Scottish Aviation Twin Pioneer that was brought in for a major inspection. This aircraft was flown to us from Sierra Leone, in Africa. The Maintenance Manual for the whole aircraft was no bigger than a modern day car Owner's Manual. The aircraft seemed very basic and we were surprised to note that chains were used to operate many of the aircraft's systems.

We were asked to work on the engines of the Pioneer, which also involved removing the two propellers and fitting new ones. The new props arrived with us simply packed and boxed and when we looked inside they were disassembled. With no instruction manuals or construction guidance it fell to us to put them together correctly and fit them to the engines. This was a great test of our knowledge and background experience at the time and we were mightily grateful to the many and various mentors who 'showed us how' over the years.

Once we had finished the refit we 'ground tested' the aircraft only to find that we couldn't achieve the required brake pressure as stated in the small Maintenance Manual i.e. 3000 p.s.i, the maximum we could achieve was 2800. The brake system was cable operated and the only adjustment possible to make was by means of tightening the cable turnbuckle, which we did, to its maximum. Once at the maximum tension we could achieve and finding the p.s.i was still too low we really only had one option left and this was to shorten the turnbuckle. So hacksaws in hand we took off about a quarter of an inch from each end of the turnbuckle. To our delight, on testing this time we found we had achieved the correct pressure, as per the Maintenance Manual.

However, our congratulations to each other were short lived as when the Pilot arrived to do the 'flight test' (who just happened to be the Scottish Aviation Chief Test Pilot who had flown every Twin Pioneer that had ever been built) he took our aircraft up for a test flight. Upon his return he said he was thrilled with the performance, he said there was only one problem, the brake pressure is too high. We told him we had had problems setting it correctly but eventually managed to get the Maintenance Manual's correct pressure as shown, to which he replied "you should not have bothered lads, none of these aircraft ever make that pressure, they're always lower". If you'd been there you would have heard the rush of air escaping from our puffed-up chests as we deflated at this stark realisation. So, to add insult to injury, we ordered a new turnbuckle and put it back as it was, low psi and all! They say you live and learn don't they? Well we certainly did that day.

As mentioned the said Twin Pioneer was the property of Sierra Leone Airways, which by this time had become one of our group of companies. I don't think the aircraft had a happy ending, and I believe its final demise occurred when it ran out of fuel and crashed in some foreign fields I guess; at least that's how the story came back to us.

Chapter 28

On another occasion I was lined up for a further adventure, this time to Vienna, Austria. We had a contract for Austrian Airlines that lasted a couple of weeks. This time another engineer, Sid Storford, came with me, Sid had been based for a long time in Germany, we got on very well together and shared the workload evenly.

The aircraft we used for this contract was a Viscount 736 series and just refuelling it was an extremely complicated process when you consider, the Viennese fuel tankers measured fuel in litres, the aircraft gauges measure in kilograms, the aircraft drip sticks measure in inches, which you converted the inches to gallons using a conversion chart and the technical log must be filled in using imperial gallons! Note to reader here, calculators had not been invented yet, it was possible to make the required calculations using a slide rule but this was extremely hard work or as a last resort, you could simply use pen, paper and brain power to work it out in longhand and don't forget we had to work out the specific gravity of the fuel as well.

When flying with this aircraft the Captain and First Officer were BUA staff and the cabin crew were all from Austrian Airlines. Our route was Vienna, Stuttgart, Paris and London. We took it in turns, Sid and myself, to fly with the aircraft each day.

Whilst in Vienna I remember going along with Sid to the Austrian Airlines maintenance hangar to ask if we could get a radio VHF set repaired. What was quite noticeable to us was that everyone in the hangar wore overalls including the Chief Engineer that was in stark contrast to our home hangar procedure. We also took particular notice of the way they managed to get some of their larger aircraft into the hangar. Their method was to inflate the nose landing gear oleo strut, which in turn raised the nose and thereby lowered the tail allowing the aircraft to slip into the hangar. It's good to see how others doing the same or a similar job manage their workload, there is usually something to be learned and we were all for that.

The Foreman took us to the Radio Workshop where one of their guys repaired the set for us. In those days valves were used inside radio sets and when ours was returned to us we noticed not only had the damaged valve been replaced but all of the valves had been likewise replaced and each one had Austrian Airlines stamped on it. We did wonder if we would get into trouble for this later on when perhaps the set was eventually disassembled back at Gatwick but no one ever said anything to us about it and Austrian Airlines didn't charge us either. Before we left we gave

181

the workshop guys some money for their weekly 'tea swindle' as a thank you.

My next notable experience was a spell spent in Cairo as 'Station Engineer'. This temporary elevation in job title came about because the permanent engineer, George Swetman, had to return to the U.K due to sickness. This station was under the control of Airwork on behalf of Sudan Airways and as such all our licences at that time had to have Sudanese dispensation before we could certify any work on their aircraft.

As part of this job I flew with the aircraft to Beirut, Khartoum, back to Cairo where I stayed whilst the aircraft flew onto London.

Airwork crews operated this aircraft and I remember one morning when I had finished refuelling and clearing up all the odds and ends the Captain and First Officer walked on board. The Captain said "Oh are you the replacement engineer" to which I replied "yes Captain and my name is ......" He replied "mine is Bell, Captain Bell but just call me Dinger old chap" then the First Officer said call me "horse". That was the start of a very good series of flights with these two officers.

Digressing for just a moment, some may wonder why the nickname 'horse'? Well all I can say is that in my experience, back in the good old days, many nicknames and sayings were used for all manner of things and people, it's just how it was then.

I recall that one chap Bill Baker at Gatwick always called everybody 'EF' he would say such things as 'how are you today EF? Or what you doing EF'? As some of you may remember, this particular catchphrase was taken from the BBC Light Programme's 'Take it From Here' series, a radio sketch within the programme called "The Glums". The Glums were a working class family who lived out their daily humdrum lives in a way that told the tale of many and various comic situations. Take it From Here was aired for the first time in 1948 and finished in 1960. It was the highlight of many relaxing family evenings around the radio following a hard day's work. The programme was written by Frank Muir and Denis Norden, both of whom some of you will remember as prolific and very funny writer's and participants of numerous sketches. The family GLUM consisted of Mr Glum, a slight dour father with a very wily outlook on every situation but in a very obvious way, he was played by Jimmy Edwards. His son, Ron, was played by Dick Bentley, and portrayed a very thick individual who was either the butt of any joke or the fall guy in most situations. Ron's wife was played by Joy Nicholls and was called 'EF' (short for Ethel) in the script, a character almost as dim as Ron but who somehow whether by luck or design, always managed to foil the dastardly, under-the-counter intrigues of the rest of the family. Arrrh, I remember it well! So sorry for my run of nostalgic flashbacks but it's amazing how they can be triggered by a simple name or saying such as 'EF'. Looking back to those days, I don't think anyone seemed to take notice or offence at these kinds of catchphrases. It might be different these days; I think the various forms of media would have a 'field day' if the same kind of sayings and name-calling was still common place.

Anyway, back to business, during my time in Cairo I stayed at a large hotel in the city not far from the Cairo Museum. One morning at breakfast I noticed a chap sitting at a table on his own, he looked very much like John Cunningham, the Chief Test Pilot for De Havilland, I knew that the Comet was on trials there at that time and so it could easily have been him, aviation was quite a small world in those days.

Whilst our Viscount was on its way to London, I spent my time wandering around Cairo, just on my own, ducking in and out of the various souks. I even went to the museum!

One lasting impression of this trip, which has always struck me as funny was the fact that to enter the airport, as a worker, you would pass through a small gate and only once you were Airside would the Guard ask you for ID. All I ever had to show in this respect was my Passport and the airline uniform I stood up in. It seemed that the wearing of a uniform was sufficiently acceptable as ID and every time I went through this gate (sometimes 4 or 5 times a day) the same Guard, I'm not sure they had another one, would ask me for my ID. As always, I would show my Passport, smile and go through, never once did he let me in without checking my Passport, strange!

Another recollection was of one of the flights into Beirut where we were given clearance to land but had to follow a helicopter in. We were getting mightily close before the helicopter got out of the way.

My only disappointment on the Cairo trip was that the actual Sudan Viscount that was painted so beautifully in Blue and Yellow was at Gatwick on maintenance and I was using one of the 831 series Viscounts fleet painted in the BUA livery. Nevertheless I had a marvellous time.

One unforgettable trip, but possibly for all the wrong reasons, was from Gatwick to Nice and onto Rome. When we landed in Rome we found one of the toilets had packed up so it was my job to remove it from the aircraft, take it apart, fix and reinstall it. So it was that I found myself sitting on the tarmac alongside the aircraft working on the loo with people walking up and down past me. The smell was something to behold, that's the toilet, not the people, I think! Anyway we took off to return home as a massive thunderstorm was building. At that time our Viscount had no such refinement as weather radar fitted and the crew had a real struggle trying to find a way around the storm.

Back at Gatwick the airline Silver City had joined us bringing with them the Bristol Freighter and Handley Page Hermes aircraft. Two people of note also came along with them, the first of which was Eddie Edger and the second Fred Ansell.

By this time the company Overseas Aviation had gone bust and we had taken over the wooden hangar together with the lads from Silver City who used to service the Hermes aircraft in that hangar, ably assisted by our own staff, which of course included me. The Hermes aircraft were not around for long and were eventually broken up. One finished up in front of Hangar 1, near to the A23 London/Brighton Road and was used by Cabin Crew for training.

A light hearted anecdote I recall regarding the Hermes aircraft, before they were broken up, was that, beyond the original Transair Hangar and Morton's Hangar, just to the west stood a small orchard and on this occasion when the Hermes aircraft was being pushed back away from the mouth of the wooden hangar they couldn't manoeuvre the tail of the aircraft past one of the trees so they had to get a couple of axes and chop the tree down.

Another experience for me, soon after we took on the Bristol Freighters was when I was on night shift my boss said "that Freighter over there has got a mag drop. Nip out, run the engines and clear it". I told him "I have never run an engine on one of those, in fact I have never been inside the aeroplane". Pete Peters turned around to me and said, "well now is the time to go and learn lad". So off I traipsed, on my own out to the aircraft which already had an electrical start truck connected. I climbed inside the fuselage of the aircraft and up the ladder to the cockpit. I looked all round the cockpit to find where the switches were and, well, to cut a long story short, I managed to start the engine and clear the defect. Whilst I was still sitting in the cockpit the Captain turned up, his name was Eric Rowley. He had his brief case with him and a whole load of blankets, curiosity overcame me and I asked him what the blankets were for. He told me he used them to wrap himself up in the cockpit in order to keep warm whilst flying. Foolishly I asked him "doesn't the aircraft have cabin heaters?" to which he replied, "oh yes but they are frightfully scary things so I won't use them".

Chapter 29

By this time we had an even greater variety of aircraft and never knew from one day to the next, which we would be working on.

Bristol Britannia outside Hangar 1 at Gatwick - Positioned in front of the blast bank (aka Mount Freeman)

The Bristol Britannia had arrived, and if I remember correctly, we had 5 of them. These aircraft had three different variants, one of which had the flight deck switches working the opposite way around to the rest of the fleet. We were told that this was because originally that aircraft was destined for Cuba. As I said before, they were the first 'all electric' aircraft. The generator control boxes were fitted in the leading edge of the wing and took 4 or 5 people to lift and slot into position.

Working outside in all weathers came as a huge challenge to us all and it was particularly difficult to ensure everything was working correctly. I remember during one engine ground run, on engine start up we couldn't get the jet pipe temperature to work this meant we weren't sure how hot the engines were getting. In an effort to solve our problem one of the instrument guys ran down the cabin and jumped up and down on the floor and believe it or not, up came the jet pipe temperature as normal, the wonders of science! On another occasion I was running the engines with a chap called Fred Malthouse, showing him how it all works. We had to simulate an engine over speed and I said to Fred "if we had a problem the engine would go to 'CUT' Fred said "it's gone to cut" and I said "no it doesn't work like that" but low and behold the engine had seized up solid.

The early jets, especially the Proteus fitted to the Britannia, had to have compressor washers, whereby you pumped fluid onto the compressor blades with the engines running, this then cleaned the blades.

We used to operate the Britannia through Entebbe and at certain times of the year millions upon millions of little tiny, what was called Lake

Flies, would be sucked into the engines and stick to the compressor blades. In fact we had one aircraft that came back from Entebbe with all 4 engines operating but they were very much down on power. We tried the standard pressure wash procedure but to no avail. One of the guys, Ray Wiggins, suggested getting the Fire Brigade to use their fire hose on the engine. This we did, I stress that I was a bystander at this time and considered it was a brave guy running those engines, but it certainly cleared the problem, the brave guys were Hugh Morgan and Junior Bashford.

We also used the Britannia on trooping flights to the Christmas Islands. It would literally be an around the world trip. They would go out in one direction and come back the other. We as engineers, found the Britannia to be a devil of a job at times to get serviceable, but once airborne they would go on and on forever. We departed one that had a generator fault on one of the engines, so we told the Flight Engineer the problem and the Crew accepted the aircraft for flight. When a couple of days later the aircraft returned to Gatwick we found the Flight Engineer had played around and reset the circuit breakers and all was well, the generator never did fail again.

The Proteus engines could sometimes be very difficult to start. They were called a 'free turbine', which in effect meant that the propeller could be turned independently of the engine. Therefore the propeller had a parking brake fitted so that when the engine was started the chap on the flight deck would need to release the parking brake. You would then hold onto the propeller in order to stop it turning until the engine began to rotate.

I recall one night on a flight departure to Sierra Leone we had a full load of passengers on board and when the crew tried to start No. 2 engine it wouldn't light up. So we were called over to solve the problem. Luckily we learnt a little trick from the guys at Aviation Traders, Stanstead, (that is where the Brits originally operated from). The trick was to remove one of the glow plugs (similar to igniter plugs) and dip a swab of cotton wool into the petrol tank of our van, then wrap the cotton wool around the plug, we then refitted the plug ready to start the engine. Please bear in mind here that the jet pipe (exhaust pipe) runs over the top of the wing on this aircraft.

By this time we had put the passenger steps back up to the forward cabin door so we could speak to the crew and let them know what we were about to do. When we were ready we signalled to the crew to start the engine. This time it lit up and as the engine started the hot gases ignited the residue of un-burnt fuel which lay in the jet pipe (remember, the exhaust pipe is over the wing?)

This resulted in a massive flame shooting out of the jet pipe reaching all the way back along the side of the aeroplane almost to the tail. Sounds horrific doesn't it, but not so, this wasn't dangerous in the sense that the aircraft would catch fire but it was a vastly spectacular display for all who viewed it against the night sky! Well I say all, but in reality no, not for one passenger who was sitting on the left hand side of the cabin and who happened to witness the whole scene first hand. He was last seen shooting out of his seat like a cannon ball, running out of the cabin onto and down the forward passenger steps and onto the tarmac shouting, "I'm not flying on that thing" eventually disappearing into the Terminal building never to be seen again. Well, what was his problem?

We departed the aircraft that night with his suitcase still in the freight hold I wonder if he ever got it back?

MOVING ON THEN... When we first received the Britannia aircraft from Stanstead approximately half a dozen of their engineers relocated to Gatwick with them, they were all great guys. I remember one, an Avionic Engineer called Taff Heinz who was quite a character. On one occasion when we were all in the canteen together having our meal, Taff jumped up onto the table and started quoting a whole series of different stories. That was the kind of guy he was, impulsive.

Another time on night shift we were in the Line Office, this was a small area in the middle of the hangar where for the most part we were based in the times before we were given an office down at the Ramp (Terminal).

Inside the office there was a large white board upon which all the aircraft registrations together with the state of play in each case was written, that is to say such information as to whether the aircraft was serviceable or unserviceable or away from base. In short, this one board displayed all of the daily operations of the fleet. Taff, in the middle of a heated argument with one of the other supervisors, grabbed a piece of cloth and proceeded to wipe the entire board clean! We understood later that the argument between the two had been about a mathematical problem. After composing himself for a moment or two, Taff, without further ado, began to write up all of the equation on the board. As you can imagine, this episode caused chaos for a while.

We had other characters among these engineers, Don Bennett. There was an expression Don liked to use frequently, 'big deal', he used it as a suffix to almost everything he did or said, "That's not a big deal". Another engineer in our team was Arthur Lacey and he sported a long white beard.

Arthur had been working with us on inspection for about six months when he came into work one day having shaved his beard off - nobody recognised him at all, not even our Deputy Chief Inspector.

One final character I would like to mention was a very good friend of ours, Mr B Debansi. He was of Indian extraction, which was something we all joked with him about that he came from Cardiff and had never seen or even set foot in India in his whole life, he liked that. When he first introduced himself he would always say "call me Bom Debansi, not Ban Debombsi" to enjoy this joke fully you have to remember our first introduction to Bom was around the time when the Aldermaston Marches were taking place and demands were being made for the 'H Bomb' to be banned. We did see his point. He also said to us if you ever see me in the terminal building or public places don't shout out Bom just wave your arms about.

Chapter 30

As time slipped by at the Airport it was decided that the three 804 series Viscounts we had should be sold. Arrangements were made to sell all three to the Polish National Airline called LOT.

Prior to sale these aircraft were brought into our hangar, one by one in order to receive their final maintenance checks, repainting in their new owner's livery and for any required modifications to meet their standard specifications.

As part of their handover procedure the Polish Airline sent some of their engineers and aircrew to us for courses, hands on engineering experience and crew training. In addition they also sent one other chap who, we understood, was a Lecturer at the Warsaw Aeronautical College.

The standard flap system on Viscounts was 'chain operated' so when the flaps were extended fully downward for landing, it was easy to take hold of the trailing edge of the flap with your hand and wobble the whole thing around. This, neither the Polish engineers nor their Lecturer had ever seen before. The Lecturer chappie seemed so intrigued by this innovation that it became his practice every morning to come into the hangar, take hold of the flap trailing edge and wobble it around. This he always followed with much shaking of his head, I think in disbelief as he walked away from the aircraft.

We were surprised to note that there were some other, quite basic, functions of the aircraft and its' normal maintenance requirements that seemed to puzzle or alarm the Polish engineers. One of which were the panels fitted to the underside of the wing leading edge and they were secured with rivets. It was quite normal for these rivets to work loose and produce a small slick of oil from around the rivet head. The Polish engineers found this hard to understand and insisted we change all the rivets as they considered that they must be loose which might result in the panels falling off.

Another item of concern for the Polish team was the brown stains seen on the fuselage around the rivet heads and pressurisation discharge valves. We had to explain to them that on early-pressurised aircraft as passengers smoked cigarettes in the cabin nicotine stains would form at these points and this was in fact what they were seeing. Sounds implausible now but it was true then. The discharge valves used to get stuck with a gooey sort of brown mess. For our part, we were very pleased when later on smoking was banned on aircraft altogether.

Finally the day came when the first aircraft was to be delivered to the Polish Airline and five of us went with it to Poland. Those selected to go were our Chief Inspector, Chief Draughtsman, Chief Training Captain Charles Coates along with John Layton and myself from the shop floor. Our reason for accompanying the aircraft was threefold, to deliver the aircraft safely to its new owners, ensure a smooth handover and to answer any and all questions the Polish engineers had, all this in the interests of international detente!

However, it soon became apparent that very little of the above would be accomplished. For as soon as we touched down in Warsaw floodlights and cameras everywhere surrounded us. We were quickly ushered into a large room where we were sat at a table adorned with a Union Jack flag at one end and a Polish flag at the other, it felt like we were about to take part in a high level International Summit or something.

I'm not sure if the next part of my story actually takes place at International Summits but we were given a meal, plied with copious quantities of Vodka after which we were eventually scooped up and taken to our hotel. At the hotel our Passports were confiscated and we were told we had to change our money into local currency. The hotel arranged all of this. The hotel management then told us that we could not leave the hotel, under any circumstances, without an escort. It felt so alien!

And so it was, the next three days we spent in Warsaw we never saw the aircraft nor were we allowed to visit the hangar. We were escorted everywhere. However on one day, I think they may have judged us as harmless to the State by then, they did take us to visit LOT's Headquarters to see their Chief Engineer. One thing we noticed and it seemed strange to us was the fact that nearly everybody went to work on bicycles.

We were taken out sightseeing to witness the rebuilding of the Warsaw ghetto areas following WWII. We visited other sights too. This latter part of our trip was very informative, interesting and very impressive.

When the time came to leave we were told to leave any local currency at the Airport, so it was a case of use it or lose it. Our flight back to London was via Amsterdam on an Illusion IL-18 turbo prop aircraft. This trip was an extraordinary experience for me and my lasting memory is that everyone we met, including the crew on the aircraft were very friendly, kind and helpful and they were very proud of their achievements.

The only downsides following our trip were that I couldn't bring myself to drink Vodka for quite some time and I found I could happily go without the huge volumes of beetroot soup with which we had been energetically served. In fact, I can report that I have never eaten beetroot soup since that time. Life in Poland at that time was a whole different world and could not be compared to anything I had ever known or experienced at home.

Chapter 31

Our next new aircraft, well new to us anyway, was the DC6B. We acquired 3 in all from Hunting Clan. In readiness for their arrival four engineers (of which I was one) were sent on a course held in Southend in order to learn about the engine of the DC6 which was a Pratt & Whitney 2800. The course ran for 3-days.

On the first day the instructor did not turn up until after lunchtime so all four of us just sat in the classroom doing nothing. When he finally arrived he apologised profusely saying that his racing pigeons had arrived home late! That's a good one we thought.

He then opened the session by saying "well you're all Licensed Engineers" and showed us where the appropriate books and slides were kept and said he would be late tomorrow as he had a hospital appointment. Not sure if he noticed an element of surprise on our faces at his course content but he concluded this 'eye-opening' session by saying "well, as you are all qualified so you most likely know as much as I do anyway", so if you get the books out, go through them using the slides and a projector, I'll see you tomorrow, as soon as I can make it.

The third day was a little more 'hands-on' and was spent in the hangar familiarising ourselves with the aircraft. In the late afternoon a flight engineer showed us how to start the engines, and this was the sum total of our 3-day course and with that we were presented with our Full Inspection Approval.

Over the next few years I spent a good deal of time working on the DC6. I never took the airframe course, which made some of my work a bit more difficult, but I must say I liked this aeroplane a lot.

On this aircraft starting the engine was normally a two-man job. Only one person could quite easily start the left hand engines. However, not so for the right hand engines, which were a little more difficult due to the fact that once the starter motor had been engaged and the propeller blades started to rotate, it was necessary to count 18 rotations of the propeller blades before the ignition system should be initiated. If working alone, I found it much easier to stand between the two-crew seats and lean forward so I could see the right hand engine out of the cockpit windows. The reason for counting the blades was to prevent engine damage due to what was known as hydraulicing. This was the effect of oil sitting in the bottom cylinders of a radial engine.

Don't get me wrong here; work in those days was usually interesting, even exciting but also fun. Having said that, we always worked with safety in mind both for each other and ourselves and great care was taken of the equipment whatever it was we were using. This point in time fell long before the formal 1974 Health & Safety at Work Act and so the only guidelines we had to follow were those of "Common Sense" given to us at home by our families, school by our tutors and at work by our mentors and supervisors. We seemed to survive perfectly well just the same.

So, what do I mean by fun at work? Well, we had some guys working with us for a while on their Work Experience. They were originally from the Civil Aviation Authority in West Africa.

One day Eddie Edger and I were in the cockpit of a DC6 carrying out the engine runs following a service check in the hangar. At that time, whilst operating the aircraft systems we noticed three of these guys walking across in front of our aircraft onto the tarmac holding up their umbrellas against the sheeting rain. To appreciate the joke, you have to understand that the DC6 was equipped with a propeller that could be put into reverse pitch, which had the effect of slowing the aircraft on landing.

As we watched the three walking ahead of our aircraft, Eddie who was sitting in the right-hand seat looked at me and we said together "yes, let's do it", at the same time we slipped each propeller into reverse pitch and we watched as the resultant slip stream/rain chased the three across the tarmac blowing their umbrellas inside out. I have to add here this caper was tempered with care as we ensured that we were careful not to use too much power but just enough to blow their umbrellas inside out. Luckily, all three of them saw the funny side of it and started jumping up and down and waving their fists at us. After we finished the engine runs and later back in the hangar, the three guys came up to us and it was hugs all round as they told us it was a good story they could tell back home.

Interested and excited we arrived for night duty in the winter time to find a note in the Inspection Office handover saying, please carry out ground runs on DC6 and complete aircraft for service, as it was too dangerous during the daytime to do the engine runs due to snow and ice on the tarmac and too many parked aircraft.

Once again Eddie and I were working this night shift (Eddie was very experienced on piston engine aircraft having come from Silver City with the Hermes). On consideration of the note and the problem, we agreed to remove the chocks from the main wheels and let the aircraft slide if it wanted to. We removed all the equipment from around the aircraft, shut the aircraft doors and got the lads on the ground to pull the aircraft steps out of the way as we carried out the engine runs. We were fortunate enough not to cause any damage as the aircraft gradually slid across the tarmac.

As mentioned previously, we used to run aircraft engines without contacting the Control Tower, as it was not deemed necessary in those days. However, on this occasion we had a DC6 positioned by the blast bank with its tail protruding over the grass; therefore the perimeter track was about 100 yards away from us.

On this day I was running the engines with another chap called Eddie Tyler, an electrician. We were going to balance the generators, which meant the engines had to be accelerated to 1800 rpm, almost to cruising power. All of a sudden we noticed frantic waving at us from outside telling us to shut down the engines. Unbeknown to us, a Cessna Bird Dog taxied up behind us and blew over. Originally the Airport tried to blame me for this incident but eventually the Pilot of the Cessna admitted having seen the grass blowing in the slip stream and said he should have stopped. For a while after this I was known as the 'Cessna Kid'.

We used to have two DC6s flying as passenger aircraft the third operated the Africargo Service. It would carry all sorts of things from fruit to monkeys.

DC6B outside Hangar 1 angled across the grass so that we could run the engines, that's where a Cessna Bird Dog came to grief as it taxied behind us.

On Friday nights the aircraft that had been freighting all week 'Africargo' was brought into the hangar. Bearing in mind we only had Hangar 1 at that time which was built for the Viscounts. The DC6 was quite a large aircraft and the only way we could get the tail of the aircraft into the hangar was to inflate the nose undercarriage to full extension, which would lower the tail sufficiently to allow us to push the aircraft back into the hangar. By this method we just about managed to get the wings and engines under cover while the front section of the fuselage was left sticking outside. This process brought back memories of my previous trip to Vienna for Austrian Airlines where we had the Viscount 736 series aircraft.

On the Friday night the freight system would be removed from the aircraft and we would disinfect and clean it as best we could then rebuild and reconfigure the aircraft into a passenger carrier with 87 seats. Despite the extensive cleaning and disinfecting of the cabin it still had a strange old smell about it the morning. The reconfigured aircraft would be used all weekend for Inclusive Tours for Europe. On Sunday night it would be brought back in to us and we would strip it back down and reconfigure it once more back to a freighter.

The DC6 engines tended to leak an awful lot of oil; we very nearly got banned from flying into Malta because of the amount of oil it deposited on the tarmac. The oil slicks used to go across the top of the wing and then be blown onto the tail planes to the extent that you could actually find oil dripping off of the elevators. Some were so bad in this respect that it was possible the engine could run out of oil before it ran out of fuel.

Departing a DC6 aircraft for service was a nail biting experience; they would sometimes come back from the end of the runway with magneto problems. There was an ignition analyser fitted to the aircraft, quite a clever bit of kit, provided it had been set up properly. Once correctly set diagnostics were relatively simple, you could pinpoint the exact offending cylinder/sparking plug very quickly

However, if the person who completed the last engine change had happened to slip up by incorrectly setting the analyser, when we viewed the diagnostic screen (a six inch square window) you could watch the electronic pulses as they checked the system, rather like the screens we see in hospitals today which monitor the heart and other organs and bodily processes. If the analyser had been incorrectly set then you would be looking at the wrong sparking plug or wrong bank of cylinders and this of course could cause huge delays and extra work.

Turning back for a moment to the matter of 'departures', the DC6 was one of the first aircraft to have a rotating red beacon with micro switches fitted to the undercarriage. Micro switches fitted to the undercarriage activated it. When the aircraft was on the ground the red beacon did not rotate but as soon as the weight started to lift off from the undercarriage the beacon would rotate. By now we had learnt that when this happened it meant we had time to jump into our van and disappear down to the canteen for dinner. We knew we had at least an hour before the aircraft would return to landing weight if, for any reason it had to return.

Chapter 32

I remember that on one particular day, when we had not had the DC6s very long it fell to one of our engineers, Des Symes, to go up into the outboard engine nacelle (rear of the engine) to inspect the air conditioning cabin compressor. As he removed the oil filter, some of the fluid splashed over his shoes. Now, Des had just bought this nice new pair of brown shoes and was wearing them for the first time so he was outraged to see all this mess. He came out of the nacelle in record time, wiped his shoes with a rag when his rage was increased ten-fold as he watched his beloved shoes turn from brown to white as the fluid stripped the top surface off.

That my friends, was our introduction to the fluid called Skydrol! The moral of this tale is 'be very careful with the purple coloured hydraulic fluid called Skydrol'. We found that apart from being the best paint stripper you could buy, it tastes disgusting, really hurts your eyes, and by the way, don't ever soak your chrysanthemums in it! To explain, when I used to grow chrysanthemum plants at home I took some into work for one of our chap's wife who had been poorly. He put them in a bucket of water to preserve them until home time but sadly they died within an hour. We later found out that the bucket was contaminated with Skydrol, so whatever you do; don't soak your chrysanthemums in Skydrol!

Turning back to the technical side for a minute if you had a problem with either the number 1 or 4 engine cabin compressor units you could disconnect them from the engine by pulling up the declutching levers behind the crew seats.

As I mentioned earlier my 3-day course on the Pratt & Whitney 2800 DC6 in Southend was skimpy to say the least and where some of the airframe/engine systems overlapped this created a bit of a problem at times, and a big learning curve.

For instance, during our first or second attempt at starting the engines following a hangar visit (service check); on a cold and wet day we had all the passenger doors closed the only open areas were the sliding Direct View or DV windows in the cockpit. As we started the engines and unbeknown to us, someone had fiddled with the cabin pressure controller so as soon as the engines picked up speed the two DV windows slammed shut and the aircraft started to pressurise.

An American company called Air Research made the pressure controller and as we were only familiar with the British Normalair systems as used on the Viscount and Brits, we weren't sure how the American system worked. We had to scramble together our best guesses as to how to depressurise the aircraft quickly. We figured out that the best way was to de-clutch the cabin compressors, which we did and the aircraft depressurised rapidly. However, we didn't escape entirely without consequence from this as one of our engineers, Ken, collapsed on the floor with a nosebleed. As I say, you live and learn and sometimes by trial and error!

The DC6 operated with 145 octane rated petrol, purple in colour, and we did have a few exhaust fires on start-up but nothing serious as it was possible to blow the flames out quickly by engaging power from the engine. The cabin heating system and de-icing systems came under the heading of Janitorial systems they were petrol driven and as such we were very wary of them during testing on the ground. They did however have their own fire detectors and extinguishing systems incorporated within them.

Being an Engineer and a human being, it sometimes happened that you got things wrong or you made a judgement that subsequently went pear shaped. I had one such incident when a DC6 came in from a flight and the Crew reported that one of the engines was running a bit rough. We completed all of the required checks and inspections, ran the engine and couldn't find anything wrong so we completed the Tech Log as 'no fault found, satisfactory for service', this was quite similar to modern day reports on computers fitted into cars in that unless there is, what's known as a hard fault, they can't find anything wrong and therefore tell you to carry on driving. So, we declared the aircraft serviceable but low and behold, on the very next take-off from Gatwick, the next day, the engine failed due to a bent push rod and there was no way we could have seen it. This kind of situation made us feel somewhat idiotic and slightly guilty at having caused a passenger flight delay. However, we soon rectified this fault with a cylinder change, which in itself was every bit as difficult as a complete engine change.

Another situation I remember was when we noticed that one of the aircraft had traces of metal in the oil filter and as a result a restriction of 50 hour repeat inspection had been applied to it. This situation continued for a couple of months and caused quite a lot of hassle. Eventually, one morning our Chief Engineer called me over and said "take Eddie Edger with you and run that engine, and do whatever you like but by the time you've finished the engine must be either declared serviceable or you've wrecked it, we cannot live with this restriction". We didn't wreck the engine but we were able to declare it serviceable. This was the only time in my career that I was actually told I could wreck something.

By this time, British United Airways was in the process of buying new VC10 and BAC 1-11

Aircraft and accordingly we were required to attend various courses on these aeroplanes. The list had been drawn up as to who would be attending which course and was placed on the board in the Inspection Office. Before embarking on these courses however, the new aircraft engineering section was expanded in another direction in that we installed a Planning Office. I remember the first job being planned by that Department was a propeller change on one of our Dakotas. We removed the old propeller and were about to put the replacement on when there came a few minutes frantic conversation between us and our new planners, they said "sorry but we called off the wrong propeller". So we had to put the original prop back on the aeroplane and changed the one on the other engine, what is the saying; best laid plans of mice and men!

Before we move into the 'Pure Jet Age', I would like to reflect upon the various types of aircraft I worked on between 1955 and 1964.

I start off with the DC3 (Dakota), Vickers Viking, Bristol Freighter, Decca Valletta, DC6, Lockheed Constellation, Viscount 708, 736, 804, 831 and 833, Dart Herald, Bristol Britannia 309, 313, 317, Fokker Friendship, D.H. Chipmunk, Aero Commander, HP Hermes and a Twin Pioneer.

In the list above there are a few I have not talked about and will do so now. Firstly, the Dart Herald. I was on night shift one night when a Dart Herald was towed to our hangar, it wasn't one operated by us and I believe it had been on tour to South America. It was reported as having a fuel system problem on the right hand engine. My boss said, "you go out and fix it" when I replied well "I have never worked on one of these before", he replied, "nor has anyone else and your engine licence covers that Dart engine, so go out and fix it". At length, I managed to fix the problem, a faulty fuel control unit. Just another steep learning curve!

Another from my list above is the Fokker Friendship with a Dart 527 engine it was brought in to us with exactly the same sort of problem. Having learnt on the previous aircraft this one we managed to fix promptly.

Both of the above aeroplanes were awkward to service and test during ground runs due to their high wings and long undercarriages. When we took the engines up to take off power on the ground the whole aeroplane would shake and bounce around consequently we found it virtually impossible to read the gauges.

The D.H. Chipmunk belonging to Sir Peter Masefield (who was at that time was one of our directors and used to fly himself around just about everywhere) and one day taxied down to our hangar. We would of course make a bit of a show and run out and marshal him in and help him out of the aircraft. He would give us half a crown between us (about 12½ p in today's money) by way of a tip. We found him to be a very nice chap and always very polite.

The Aero Commander we serviced belonged to the Guinness family and would be parked at the hangar for us to check the oils etc.

Chapter 33

Whilst I have been merrily working away on aircraft the Planning Department has started to expand and take on more staff, one of these happened to be young lady who started in September 1962, working as a Secretary to Mr Everett, the Production Planning Engineer, I had, over a period of time, seen her walking around but I'd never spoken to her.

At this time rapid changes were taking place in the airline business too and as a result we were asked to attend quite a few courses in order to fully equip ourselves to work on the new VC10 and BAC 1-11aircraft.

In 1963, I attended my first course and this was a two-week course based at Rolls Royce, Derby. The course covered all aspects of the Conway engine as fitted to the VC10 aircraft. On my return to work I went straight back maintaining the existing fleet.

I used to play a lot of golf in those days and all of my partners were members of staff, some I remember were Robbie Warren, Eddie Tyrer, Des Symnes, Ted Bath, Gerry Clifton and Mick Cotgreaves. I had finished work on one particular afternoon in May 1963 and before I went off to play golf, I parked my car behind the aforementioned young lady's car when all at once she appeared; I plucked up courage and asked her out. She said her name was Rosemary and she agreed to go out with me. To cut a long story short, we were married in June 1966, and here we are some 56 years later writing this book together, that is to say me drafting and Rosemary typing.

The next course I was asked to attend covered the VC10 Airframe. It was a six-week course based mainly at Gatwick with weekly trips to Weybridge to see the aircraft in build. I must admit that I found both of these courses quite challenging as they encompassed a great deal of new technology. During the VC10 Airframe course, I remember the instructor who taught the section on air conditioning system said that when he got to this section where he is talking about refrigeration packs which are fitted in the leading edge of the wings, he began to question why on earth he was going into such detail, because in his view, he doubted whether any one of us would understand. I must say we found that quite reassuring as none of us did!

Another course I attended, in August 1963 covered the Rolls Royce Spey engine and this too meant two weeks in Derby. I recall the course information being quite restricted in some areas because at this point in time the engines were still being tested, so I guess they gave us all they had.

My training course on the BAC 1-11 Series 200 started just after the fatal crash of the prototype 1-11 where unfortunately the entire flight test crew were killed. We were told however the course would still go ahead and we would be instructed on how the aircraft was designed and built before the accident. We were also told that they would be holding a 'differences course' once BAC had ironed out all the problems and successfully tested them. The course for the most part was held at Gatwick but also involved us travelling by coach, once a week, to Hurn Airport, Bournemouth. This was quite a long trip and most of the day was spent travelling. So it did not leave a great deal of time to look around the factory, however, over the duration of the course we did actually learn quite a bit.

Once I had finished the courses it was well over a year before the new aircraft arrived so in the meantime it was back to DC3s, Viscounts, Brits and DC6s etc. but still trying to maintain all the information we had gathered over the preceding months.

Chapter 34

Our engineering way of life had changed a lot since the 1950s, gone were the days of 'single traded' engineers such as 'Electrical', 'Instrument' or 'Radio'. All of these trades had now been amalgamated into what was now known as 'a multi X licence' and were re-classified as Avionic Staff.

In our case, working for BUA, this meant that some Avionic Staff were promoted to 'Chargehands'. This represented a huge shift in workload, as there was much more electronics work undertaken.

Although the Engine and Airframe trades were gradually merging, we found that the people with those basic skills still tended to work on their strongest subjects. My Inspection Approval at that time encompassed engine and airframe category A & C on all aircraft operated by the company and their customers. This level of approval enabled me to work on other operator's aircraft as and when the need for assistance arose. Just to give a 'for instance', an Air Ferry DC4 was on one of the departure stands when an engine defect was reported. Due to this higher level of approval, I together with a couple of fitters were able to quickly rectify the fault while the aircraft was still at the terminal.

BUA Engineering went through some difficult times in the 1960s. Freddie Laker was Managing Director of the company and he insisted that any pay negotiations would only be entered into collectively. This resulted in immediate Unionisation for us all.

Those of us who were Inspectors or Chargehands joined, what was known at that time as the White Collar Union headed up by Clive Jenkins. However, the lads on the shop floor were AEU. There were very many arguments during negotiations in an attempt to achieve parity on wages with the Corporations. This concluded with Fred sacking us all because we had gone on an overtime ban. However, following further talks our notices were withdrawn.

Then a while later the arguments resurfaced; but this time resulting in strike action. What I remember most about the strike was how very cold it was just standing around on picket duty. A huge amount of bad feeling was generated when we found out that aircrew had been asked to work on the engineering side. The strike lasted three or four long weeks and at the end of it we found that we no longer worked for BUA but had been transferred into Aviation Traders. The airline remained BUA it was just engineering that was changed. This move caused an awful lot of bad feeling.

The lead-up to the strike was nasty. One of our engineers, Fred Malthouse, was marshalling a Britannia onto the tarmac outside of the hangar, aircrew were taxiing the aircraft when all of a sudden Freddie Laker appeared, and rushing out of the hangar he pushed the engineer out of the way and marshalled the aircraft himself. The next day there were pictures of Freddie Laker, if I remember it correctly, Freddie standing in front of the Britannia with a caption reading 'Boss marshals his own aircraft'. I have often wondered if this had been a PR stunt.

Another incident was when some of the lads wanted to undo work they had already done on an aircraft, one or two wanted to write really difficult defects down on the sheets all in an effort to delay the aircraft going back into service. When we returned to work after the strike the atmosphere was no better, there was so much bitterness between senior management and staff, which took a very long time to heal. It was certainly a time I did not enjoy.

At that time of the strike the BAC 1-11 was late into service but this was due to the prototype crash and development issues with the production aircraft, but the company put small notices on the back of the Viscount passenger seats saying words to the effect that due to Industrial Action by the engineering staff we are having to use Viscount aircraft instead of the BAC 1-11.

Fred left his post as Managing Director in 1965 and Max Stuart Shaw followed him for a couple of years. Max just oversaw the new colour scheme of Sandstone and Blue; he then left and was followed by Alan Bristow who fairly quickly changed us back to BUA Engineers.

It's true to say that we did not know what to expect with Alan Bristow, him being a Helicopter specialist, but we soon found out. He called everyone into the Viscount hangar and stood on a bench, introduced himself by saying he had been asked to make British United Airways profitable or close it down, as you can imagine, that went down well. He was an entirely different character to Fred. Fred we felt was very much a 'showman'. Our Boss prior to Freddie Laker, a Mr Lewindon, we hardly ever saw and when we did he didn't speak to anyone. My only recollection of him was when we night stopped in Las Palmas on route to Accra. He flew from Gatwick with us as he was on a business trip to Las Palmas. As we night stopped he joined us for dinner and during the evening he asked 'what was the noise on the outside of the aircraft whilst in flight'. I was able to tell him it was due to the fact that one of the letters stuck on the side of the fuselage had worked itself loose and was banging against the side of the aeroplane, so nothing serious.

Something that no longer happens on commercial airlines these days (particularly since now they have built in In-flight entertainment) is the regular requirement for configuration changes to the aircraft cabins. We were forever removing seats, converting the aircraft from a passenger cabin to a freighter or perhaps adding or removing seats dependent upon the route being taken. Changes were even made if it was a scheduled service or an inclusive tour and then of course there were the trooping flights. All in all, quite a pantomime, the 'Keystone Cops' had nothing on us.

The MOD trooping contract required all passenger seats to be facing rearwards, originally we used airframe fitters to remove or install seats but the frequency of seating changes necessitated a different approach, so we set up a configuration department and took on enough extra staff to operate four shifts. Each seating plan required its' own set of drawings and it would not just be seats you moved but also bulkheads and curtains that had to be repositioned. Along with reconfiguration went seat removal for what we called 'deep cleaning' or repair. These seats would be placed into our own seat bay awaiting attention. This turned out to be quite a hive of industry. As mentioned above these work patterns continued right up until the introduction of wide body aircraft with built in entertainment.

Hangar 3 was built in the early 1960s, it was built in two sections, and the first bay to be built was at the East end and this held the tail dock for the VC10. Our own works and bricks department did most of the construction. The only difficulty we experienced during construction was that our company ran out of money and as a consequence we used the hangar for a year without doors!

The Company was forced into building the hangar sooner than they wanted because the CAA clamped down on service checks being carried out in the open. They insisted on the aircraft being under cover.

Harking back for just a moment to aircraft seats, we used to have a full cabin service whereby the cabin crew would come around offering meal trays and drinks from a trolley. Then all of a sudden, the tour operators wanted cheaper seats so Courtline (the Airline) was the first to introduce 'Seat Back Catering' whereby a panel in the back of the seat in front of you could be opened and this contained a pack of sandwiches, top tray for outbound passengers lower tray for inbound passengers, one of the problems was hungry passengers would eat the lot leaving nothing for the return trip, to overcome this a lock was fitted to the lower compartment, however on trips that included hot climates the sandwiches for the return trip would start to curl up. This was not a very popular system with passengers so all the companies soon reverted back to the original system.

Another couple of early airline entrepreneurs in the passenger flight business at Gatwick in the early 1960s were a husband and wife operation. The husband was the Captain and his wife the Hostess. I'm not quite sure how true it is, but there was talk that they made the sandwiches at home overnight!

A second airline started up at the same time I recall was owned by a Lord somebody or other who had a Viscount aircraft. This seemed to operate for about a week and then disappeared.

My first introduction to the BAC 1-11 was one morning when in the Inspection Office the telephone rang. It was our Engineering Rep at the factory saying they are just starting up the engines, he must have held the telephone away from himself because we could all hear the loud noise of the Rolls Royce Spey engines coming to life. The Rep we had then based at Hurn was Joe Roper, a very tall easy-going experienced engineer. One story I remember about Joe was that for a time he was our Hangar 1 Foreman and one Friday afternoon when all the work was finished someone asked Joe if we could get an 'early trap' (leave before time). Joe said "yes but you must be careful, leave the hangar one at a time, at one minute intervals". By his reckoning, we worked out that the last person to leave would be about one and a half hours past normal knock off time! That was taking caution to the extreme.

There was one other small aeroplane that was used by our company in a semi-private capacity and this was a Cessna 310. The Cessna 310 was a twin-engine job and I must say we didn't do much work on it. My only involvement was the occasional taxiing of it down to the ramp prior to departure.

Chapter 35

Now the time has come for me to be introduced to our much-treasured VC10 and BAC 1-11 Series 200 aircraft. Before we received these two aircraft at Gatwick, our Engineering Management Team dispatched a couple of Licensed Airframe/Engine Supervisors together with a couple of Avionic Inspectors to Weybridge for the VC10 and to Wisley for the 1-11. These chaps were given 'hands on' experience directly from the manufactures so that when the aircraft arrived with us we did have staff possessing 'first hand' knowledge of the aeroplanes, unlike the rest of us, who had to rely on basic classroom instruction, albeit over a period of months prior to receipt.

When the new aircraft arrived, the formally trained lads were effectively put in charge and we were required to do as they told us. Overall this worked very well and it gave us a chance to learn without too much pressure being placed upon us from the outset.

The first course of action for the new aircraft was 'crew training' (no flight simulators in those days). The training was carried out by the manufactures own Test Pilots instructing our Pilots.

The first to arrive with us were the VC10s', there were two of them delivered in September 1964. The delivery was rapidly followed by a very hectic period of crew training (as detailed above), after which came demo flights. Freddie Laker, not being one to miss out on a promotional photo opportunity, took advantage of the VC10s large freight door to the cabin and loaded his silver Rolls Royce car onto the aircraft for proving flights. As we said, always a showman was our Fred.

VC10 in Nairobi on a route proving flight carrying Fred Laker's Rolls Royce. That big freight door was not always the easiest to operate and service.

The first service flight for the VC10 was a trooping flight to Aden, North Africa, in October 1964. In 1965 we acquired a third VC10. In 1968 we introduced our fourth aircraft, the prototype G-ARTA and I propose to give it a special mention later on.

The BAC 1-11 G-ASJI was handed over from the manufacturers in January 1965, this was the first of ten 200 Series aircraft.

Both the BAC 1-11 and the VC10 were very noisy aircraft in fact when the VC10 took off late on a frosty evening; the tremendous crackling sound it made could be heard for miles around. The reason the sound travelled so far was partly due to the fact of the steep climb after take-off. This was bad enough we thought, but when the BAC 1-11 aircraft arrived they were even worse. At that time they were minus an additional silencer fitted to the cowling. So, when they started night time crew training (there was no jet ban at that time) it was possible to watch as the lights came on in virtually all of the houses in Horley and people opening windows to see what on earth the noise could be.

As I mentioned earlier the MOD trooping flights were conducted with the troops onboard sitting and facing rearwards. However, that soon stopped when they were flown on the VC10 or BAC 1-11 as it was found that due to the rapid climb following take off the troops were left suspended in their seat belts. Well that was another lesson learned by trial and error!

By this time, the VC10 was all ready a well developed aircraft having been in service with BOAC previously, so luckily we had none of the teething problems and experiences that we had with the 1-11.

I remember well one evening on the ramp, I was assisting with the turnaround of a 1-11 on crew training and I had been instructed by the engineer in charge to look around the tyres for signs of wear or damage. On inspection I found one of the main wheel tyres was just about worn to limits. At that precise moment the BAC Test Pilot walked up to me and asked what was the problem and I explained we would have to replace the tyre. He looked at the tyres then put his arm round my shoulder and said "don't worry lad I have one more flight to do tonight with one landing, and I can assure you we fly with much more wear than that". With his words ringing in my ears I said, "right let's get going then" and off he went. That, for anyone interested, was Captain Hayley Bell, who was related to John Mills the actor. He was a really nice guy, like all the test pilots we had on the 1-11 and the VC10s. They gave us so much confidence it was a very special time as far as I was concerned.

Another curious example of 'what a small world aviation is' was whilst the 1-11 aircraft were going through the 'route proving' phrase, one of BAC representatives who at that time flew on the aircraft and whom I would most likely have bumped into, was in fact John Thorpe, a Flight Test Observer who also later on worked for the CAA on flight safety. Incidentally, John is now the main Committee/Organiser for the Smallfield Aviation Group of which I am happy to say, I am a member - what a small world!

Remembering my earlier comments regarding the BAC 1-11 course we attended, when we were instructed as to how the aircraft operated prior to the fatal accident. We did eventually attend a two-week 'differences course' which explained the differences in operation prior to the accident and following it. This was held at Gatwick and covered instruction on the new control system layout together with various other safety items.

One important thing I should have mentioned was that on the original 1-11 course the Instructor covering the electrical system (Arthur Warner) had himself been involved with the design of rocket systems.

He was responsible for producing the schematic drawings for the 1-11 and he drew these on the blackboard for us just from memory without the need for reference to any notes. To us his knowledge was completely amazing and we would eagerly and religiously copy his drawings from the board into our course notes.

I remember one particular morning he was completing his drawings on the blackboard when he wrote alongside them, in block letters, D.N.F.T.B.10. As we all studiously copying this, one of the chaps on the course asked what these letters stood for. He said Oh no, don't copy that it's just to remind me **'Don't forget tea break 10 o'clock'**. It's true to say, we hung on his every word and in our eyes he was an absolute genius. I think we all managed to learn much more because of his manner of instruction.

Once the 1-11 was put into service we found a few problems. We discovered that the undercarriage lights did not always function correctly. In order to analyse what was actually happening here we had to fit a test set into the system, which was supplied, to us by BAC. Another, quite serious problem was when we noticed 'main wheel shimmy' on landing. Our resolution to this problem was to hang a large weight to the front of the landing gear and this damped out the shimmy effect.

From a ground handling point of view, we found that in towing the aircraft it became easy to get the nose wheel off the ground. As a result of these findings, we always put ballast bags in the forward hold.

We also found that on the first flight of the day we were unable to start the Rolls Royce Spey engines. They would rotate but the fuel control unit would 'stick'. The fancy name for a control unit was 'Combined Acceleration and Speed Control Unit' or (CASCU). At length we managed to overcome the problem of sticking by simply opening the cowlings whilst another engineer went on board and selected engine start. Our 'very technical' method would then be to hit the side of the unit with a hide faced hammer and hey presto the engine would start! This rather protracted method was thereafter used each morning to start the engines until the CASCU was finally modified, much to our relief.

The next thing to 'play up' was the air supply system to the engine starter. There was an air shut-off valve and a pressure control valve fitted between the fuselage and engine both squeezed into a very small space. These two components regularly failed and were very difficult to change due to lack of space to work in.

Another major problem affecting the operation of these aircraft engines was the water injection system. It was necessary to inject demineralised water into the engine thereby increasing the air density, this in turn, increased engine power. Increased power was particularly important when flying African routes where airfield temperatures were extremely high and the need to lift-off quickly was important.

There were two valves fitted to these engines the first of which was the air delivery valve, this operated an amber light on the instrument panel in the cockpit indicating sufficient air pressure. The second was the water flow valve that operated a green light indicating water was flowing. The take-off sequence was as follows: Select water injection, thereby increasing engine power. Confirmation of take-off power was indicated by an amber light followed by a green light, only then was the engine power sufficiently increased for take-off. However this sequence frequently operated the other way around, i.e. the green light came on first indicating a problem! When this occurred the outcome was an engine 'flame out'. When this occurred, especially if we happened to be running the engines in the engine detuner or muffler as it was called at Gatwick, the whole aircraft would be shrouded in a white mist (steam) it quickly dispersed and caused no harm to the engineers or the aircraft

The Company had been talking to Rolls Royce in an effort to pick their brains as to how this problem might be overcome. And so it was that one night when I came into work to do my usual night shift at 22:00 hrs I found a note had been left asking me to work with a Rolls Royce representative, someone who was at that time the most experienced rep. working out of the Flight Sheds at Wisley. The note confirmed that the rep. would run the engine whilst I was to assist and observe; always happy to learn, I happily complied.

The Rolls Royce rep duly arrived (I have forgotten his name but seemed a nice chap) and we walked out together to the 1-11, which had been laid on specifically for our tests. I noticed he had a tape recorder with him that he dictated into the whole time; 'boy' did I learn what you could do to a jet engine that night, fantastic learning curve for me. As we reviewed the engines and he was making the small adjustments down on the engine, he emphasized to me how important it was that whilst 'he' could make these adjustments; 'we' (meaning our engineers) were never to touch it. I guess we must have spent the best part of two or three hours checking everything and most of the checks were at take-off power. Goodness knows what the local residents thought about the continual noise (still no jet ban).

After his work was complete the Rolls Royce rep. returned to Wisley and made his recommendations. These eventually resulted in Rolls Royce making a few adjustments to the valves, after which all was well.

There were not too many funny stories to tell relating to us working on the 1-11. It was all quite serious stuff really. However, one instance does spring to mind that was in connection with the auxiliary power unit (APU). The APU was a small gas turbine engine fitted below the fin and rudder aft of the two engines, this unit supplied air for engine starting as well as for electrical power whilst the aircraft was on the ground. A company called Garrett in America manufactured the unit and initially one of their reps, an American chap was allocated to us. During his visit we began to experience problems with the APU. Late one evening when we were talking to the rep about this particular problem and as the fault was intermittent we suggested that when we needed him to come and check for the fault, "we will come to your hotel room and knock you up". "He said "hey don't say that buddy, in American lingo that means you will make me pregnant". I remember thinking to myself at the time, wouldn't it be great to have one common language, who knows, it might have saved a few wars!

Looking back upon my experiences and working days and comparing them to practices of today, I think it's very sad to note the apparent lack of enthusiasm for new aircraft. In my day engineers would rush out of the hangar to see a new type of aircraft land or take off. Sadly this seems to have fallen by the wayside. This openness and freedom in the work place was mostly due to the fact that we didn't have the very stringent security levels that you see in place today. It is fair to say that we had a 'Security Person' (singular) who sat in his office but who was, in many ways, a jack of all trades but he certainly didn't have a Kalashnikov at his side!

Chapter 36

My Dad left Croydon Airport when it closed where he had been working on night shifts, and had managed to slot himself in very neatly to a new job working as a telephone operator for the company at Gatwick; however, it was still permanent night shift. He found himself using the manual switchboard the Company had just installed. Dad had a background in this type of work previously working as a telephone switchboard operator at the Telephone Exchange at Purley. Sometime later my dad had to make another job change, due to the Gatwick switchboard being automated. In his new job he was working as a member of a small (4 people) Security Department. His main job here was to act as, well almost as receptionist really with the occasional security walk about. It wasn't until much later that the Security Team started to fly on certain routes, bringing back containers full of diamonds and he would then accompany them on their onward journey by van to 'wherever'. Upon reaching 'wherever', he would be contacted by a courier who would relieve him of the diamonds for the next stage of their journey.

The Airport itself was completely open to visitors at weekends and it was commonplace to see employees together with their families looking around the aircraft. At Christmas time we held parties in the hangar for employees' children and one of the aircraft would be taxied to the front of the hangar where Father Christmas would climb out. These were wonderfully free and easy days, full of fun and laughter for us all. It's so very sad that we have to mourn their passing in light of modern-day security risks and fears.

Following my comments regarding enthusiasm, we did have one amusing incident where one of the VC10s was on the ramp and this was in the very early days of its operation. Robbie Jewett, one of a handpicked team tasked with certifying the aircraft, was inside the aircraft fixing defects. The aircraft was awash with staff at the time, some working, and some just looking on when the Operations Director walked through the cabin and shouted in a voice that carried above everyone else's "Everyone Off". Everyone, including Robbie who was in no mood to be mucked about as he had had very little, if any sleep over the last couple of days, promptly went home. At length the Director said to John Stone, "right now get the blokes back inside to work" to which John replied "well we can't clear any of the work because Robbie has gone home". At this realisation the Director, with a tinge of embarrassment in his voice, flew into a panic shouting, "Go and fetch Robbie and get him back here straight away". Which just goes to prove that power and authority doesn't always carry the day, especially when the 'little people' have been on nights and are knackered!

With the VC10 operation we flew to Sierra Leone once a week. On these occasions we were required to display the Sierra Leone flag, which meant removing the Union Jack, and fitting the Sierra Leone flag. The normal flight pattern was to depart late at night and on one particular occasion, and I can't honestly remember how this happened, but we forgot to change the flag from Union Jack to Sierra Leone. The aircraft started up and was taxing out when someone noticed our error. Luckily they managed to recall the aircraft and change the flag thereby avoiding an International Incident! There were some funny old rules around in those days, apparently the aircraft could have been impounded or at the very least seen as an insult.

I recall during the first winter of our operation of the VC10, Gatwick was under the influence of thick fog and as a consequence a VC10 was diverted to Heathrow. This coincided with my shift and I together with a small gang including Robbie drove to Heathrow. When we arrived at the airport it was foggy there too and we struggled to find the diverted aircraft. When we finally located it we noticed it was displaying the Sierra Leone flag on the tail so that change was our first job. A couple of lads went and found a cherry picker to assist in this change and due to the cold and fog they spent the whole night removing the old stick on flag and replacing it with a new Union Jack. They had to use bucket after bucket of hot water to warm up the flag sufficiently to allow it to be peeled off. Then came the struggle to get the new flag to stick onto the cold wet fin. What a performance! By the end of the shift the two lads were cold, tired and fed up to the back teeth. Eventually we managed to declare the aircraft serviceable then the passengers and crew soon arrived and were departed from Heathrow.

Times were changing, and eventually I came off shift work on the ramp and transferred to the hangar, this was sort of a semi promotion from Inspector to Chargehand. The role meant being in charge of all hangar engine work, in real terms this meant in charge of Hangars 1 and 3.

At this juncture my readers might feel a short break from all this aircraft talk would be a good idea. So instead I would like to mention some of the characters we had around us at that time. I propose to tell you 'as it was then' not as it is today.

In the 1950s' we had some lads from Airwork join us at Gatwick, most of who had previously worked at Gatwick's old Airport (The Beehive). Airwork had a hangar in which quite a lot of MOD work was conducted and some of the names I remember very well were Ken Funnell, he was known to everyone as 'Smokey'.

Smokey was very much a creature of habit in that he would arrive at work 10 minutes before the shift started, he would then get changed into his overalls and spend the next 10 minutes in the loo! This he did every day, of every single week, of every single year. Another name was Brian Beck, he was known as 'Becksarb' he would eat an apple for lunch with sandwiches, then go to sleep. He would often have 5 minutes sleep at tea breaks. He seemed to have the knack of taking 'power naps' and this was before they ever became fashionable for high-flying city folk!

Bill Claxton another engineer around at the time, he became a main Union Organiser in days of Freddie Laker. So far as we engineers were concerned, he ran the football swindle, by which I mean we paid into a syndicate and selected some lines on Vernons and Littlewoods Football Pools. I can't remember that we ever won anything and when Premium Bonds became fashionable he changed from doing the Football Pools to buying £1 Premium Bonds. The idea was that whatever we won would be reinvested. As you can tell we never won much otherwise I would not be writing this narrative I would be living on some tropical island soaking up the sun.

Eddie Smith, yes good old Eddie, now he used to tell a story, the authenticity of which I cannot be sure but it goes like this. He and a gang of fitters were on their way to Northolt travelling in a van in thick fog, as I have said before we used to get real thick yellow fog. Anyway, they seemed to be going around in circles and Eddie asked the driver what was happening. The driver said he couldn't seem to find the road off this roundabout. Believe it or not, they were going round someone's front garden that had a circular driveway. Yes, maybe?

George Dyke, now he was known as 'Dinker', he had an affliction that at times made his arms move rapidly. If he was eating his cheese roll at tea break when this happened his cheese roll would go in all directions much to our amusement. However, the strangest thing was that if George who was a qualified First Aider was attending someone with a needle in his hand, perhaps removing a splinter or whatever his hands were as steady as a rock.

Another one of our colleagues was Jock Neilson who lived in Brighton. One Sunday we called him into work, now I must point out here that he was a bit accident prone and a nightmare to work with, evidenced by the fact that he once drilled through a hydraulic pipe by accident. On a separate occasion he walked into the trailing edge of a set of flaps and knocked himself out. However, on this occasion Jock agreed to come in by train but being a Sunday service he was an absolute age getting into work and when he did eventually arrive he apologised for his lateness saying he had fallen asleep on the train only waking up at East Croydon. He then had to wait for a train coming back to Gatwick. His saving grace was that he was a very good engineer.

I was reminded just recently about a chap we had working at Croydon Airport, sorry I cannot remember what his job was, quite an elderly man at the time as I seem to remember; I recall he drove a van. Anyway, on behalf of the foreman he used to sit in the Transair canteen at tea breaks and at meal times. He always had with him a stopwatch and whistle and when the break time was up he would blow the whistle to get people back to work. I have often wondered if that was the origin of the term 'whistle blower'.

Chapter 37

Writing as I was earlier about the small Security Department consisting of just 4 Officers, one of whom was my Dad. I remember one of Dad's fellow officers being rather over-zealous and enthusiastic within his role. He seemed hell bent on catching anyone believed to be leaving the company after work with what he deemed as 'stolen property'. The Security Office was sited at the main entrance of Hangar 1 and was also adjacent to our clocking in/out machines. In order to clock out at the end of your shift, first and foremost you had to form an orderly queue in true British style; we love a queue. Each person stood, clock card in hand ready to push it down into the machine when your turn came to do so. You would put the card into the top slot and pull the handle at the side of it downward (rather like a modern day slot machine at the casino) thereby punching a hole in the card and at the same time endorsing the card with the time and date adjacent to the punched hole. Quite straightforward really one would think.

Now this particular Security guy took it upon himself to wander up and down the line of people looking at them all the time scrutinising them and any bags they might be holding for 'stolen' goods. One day during this process he spotted a chap in the line holding a bag that seemed, to his eyes at least, to contain something suspicious.

He asked the chap what he had in the bag; the chap replied "Oh rhubarb". The Security guy then got annoyed and said "no cheek from you, what have you got in there". Again the chap replied "RHUBARB" only this time he spoke much louder, as you can see! With this the Security guy told him in no uncertain terms what would happen to him if he were found to have stolen property in the bag. He followed this warning up with a request to see inside the bag, as you can imagine by this time everyone had their ears pinned tight to the altercation between them. The chap in the line dutifully complied with the Security guy's somewhat over-zealous request by opening the bag for all to see. All that could be seen were some rather juicy looking sticks of rhubarb! Everyone in the line of workers fell about laughing, as they watched the Security guy rather stiffly walk away sporting a very red and shiny face. I am not sure if he ever saw the funny side of it, I suspect not. But I do know my Dad never mentioned anything about it.

Jock Stewart (of cheese and butter roll fame) was another character who, if you recall, was one of our engine fitters who lived the other side of Croydon. If he worked overtime past 20:00 he would not bother catching a train home, he would sleep at work in one of the engine bay workbenches. As unbelievably far-fetched as it sounds it was true. I was on night shift one night and happened to walk through the engine bay at about 02:00, there was no one in sight; just a few hangar lights on, when all of a sudden one of the doors on the side of the workbench opened and Jock got out to go to the toilet. I am not kidding you I nearly wet myself on the spot.

INTERLUDE OVER,
BACK TO AEROPLANES!

The 200 Series 1-11 fleet was starting to build up to the 10 aircraft we had ordered, but in the meantime we had had a couple of engineers with us from, I think it was Braniff Airlines in the USA. They were working with us in order to gain experience with the 1-11 before their own order was delivered. We got the feeling they didn't like the 1-11 very much, they seemed to think it was rather messy and fiddly. We may have been wrong but that was the impression they gave us.

It was about this time, late 1964 that the airport imposed some new regulations, and part of these was that we had to call ground control to get permission to start the engines and also have the red rotating beacon operating.

We also began to feel the implications of a noise ban, which meant we couldn't carry out full power runs on engines prior to 06:00. This new rule caused us problems with regard to the early morning flights to Rotterdam and Amsterdam and other early flights. We overcame some of the restricted practice by positioning the aircraft that needed an engine run outside and ready to start the engine when the night freighter aircraft was departing. We would start the engine when we heard the freighters start up but we only carried out basic requirements i.e. checking the generators, checking for fuel and oil leaks and other minor issues. We would only run the engines at idle power, we would not call up for permission to run the engines or have any lights on, nobody ever complained but I am sure the authorities knew what we were doing.

We built engine noise mufflers so called de-tuners. We had one built for the VC10 and one for the 1-11; they were big structures that you backed the aircraft into. At the back of the de-tuner was a ramp arrangement that would deflect the exhaust gases upwards; people reckoned it dumped all the noise onto the 9th green at Ifield Golf Course. I know for a fact one evening when we ran the engines on a VC10 we dumped a set of steps into the wooden hangar the other side of the de-tuners fortunately missing all the parked aircraft.

One evening at about 18:30 I was talking to John Stone who was one of our Inspectors. He was about to run the engines on one of the 1-11 aircraft that was parked in a de-tuner. I jokingly said I was going to the canteen so please don't make too much noise. I heard the engines start quickly followed by an almighty bang. It transpired that the right hand engine had decided to fail and deposited a whole set of turbine blades around the de-tuner. Not much more to do about this type of disaster but to change the engine.

Changing the engine on a 1-11 meant that we had to phone Arnold Sheead who at that time was the Chief Engineer for him to tell us which spare engine to use. This was due to a funny old lease agreement we had with Rolls Royce and only Arnold had all the information. Even if he was at home late at night we still had to phone him, he had all the paperwork with him.

The type of maintenance we carried out on the BAC 1-11 and VC10s was such that we never had the aircraft in the hangars longer than four days at a time. Major maintenance was broken down into what was called 'not exceed' items therefore every time the aircraft came in for maintenance we did a part of the major maintenance at the same time. This worked very well; the VC10 was worked on mainly Monday to Thursday and the 1-11s Tuesday to Friday.

Chapter 38

In the early 1960s due to expansion at the airport we engaged more staff. At this time we also established a Technical Records Department to look after all the aircraft logbooks. A further department sprung up namely the Technical Library. By this time we had more technical manuals than we had ever seen before. Fortunately for us with the introduction of the 'Air Transport Association 100' format all of the manuals followed the same structure. For example, Chapter 28 in any of the manuals would detail the aircraft fuel system whilst Chapter 21 dealt with air conditioning. Previous to the ATA 100 system no two manufacturers used the same sequencing of chapters so there was no standardisation of technical information, as you can imagine this nonconformity made life unnecessarily difficult for our teams in the old days.

Although the company had expanded with a lot more aircraft, engineering numbers on the shop floor were kept to a bare minimum. I believe Senior Management thinking was that it was preferable to allow staff to work overtime and earn higher wages thereby keeping them and their families happy. This subsequently proved to be the case as there was a very low turnover of engineers and they all seemed happy with their lot.

There were three guys on the shop floor, Albert Styles, J D Edwards and Jack Urquhart who proved to be past masters at sussing-out where and when the overtime was likely to be needed. They seemed to have the knack of being in the right place at the right time. I remember well one occasion when Jack Urquhart said he would like to work on the nose leg of the 1-11, which had just arrived in the hangar for a service check. Jack and his apprentice, Bob Bedwell had noticed a problem on the nose landing gear and the Inspector agreed with their diagnosis and decided that the nose leg needed to be changed. So Jack was asked to work overtime to fix it. Well, it could have been coincidence of course?

By this time the company had started to offer full apprenticeships and a formal scheme was set up. An Inspector called Buck Ryan was promoted from the ranks to be in charge of the apprentices. We were lucky enough to engage some really very good lads to start working with us. Some of their names spring to mind, Pete Barnes, Dave Lear, Pete Hollingsworth and Stuart Evans. There were many more, too many to name them all but if they read this they will know who they are.

What I consider to be 'thinking way before its time' was the employment of two girls as avionic apprentices, Sarah Peters and Viv (sorry I forgot her surname). An early small step towards 'equal opportunities'.

The apprentices who were taken on to become airframe/engine fitters had the advantage of working on aircraft needing considerable structural work and this background stood them in good stead for later life when working on the Boeing 707s. I will mention more about the apprentices and my involvement with them as we progress through this book.

Chapter 39

Now that we were using two hangars for maintenance, Hangar 3 was now dedicated to VC10s and Britannias whilst Hangar 1 was used for 1-11s and Viscounts. Staff were now based in both hangars and seemed split into one of two categories, long haul or short haul, my role at that time involved floating between both hangars.

At this time, Freddie Laker (who had left us) was in the throes of starting up Laker Airways. In the early part of 1966 four or five of our staff members decided to leave British United and subsequently became founder members of Laker Airways. I was asked if I wanted to join them but I really enjoyed my job and could see no reason to leave, also in June of that year I was getting married, another milestone for me.

My future wife Rosemary and I had already booked Hotel Olinda on the Copacabana Beach in Rio de Janeiro for our honeymoon at a princely cost of 10 shillings a night in old money (this being the equivalent of 50p today) and had paid a deposit. Our Staff Travel tickets were also booked at a cost to us of £58 in old money and this was for the two of us, so we decided not to risk our future plans on the Laker venture, which was so uncertain.

Chapter 40

The Rolls Royce Conway engine was fitted to the VC10 aircraft and was very powerful, but noisy and burnt a lot of fuel. When we first started servicing this engine in the hangar we had to get the jet pipe area of the aircraft checked out for radiation and this was due to the altitude the aircraft flew at. Fortunately radiation of any significance was never found and the practice was soon stopped.

Our VC10s were fitted with what was known as a 'combustor system' a special method used to start engines when an external air source was not available. The system consisted of three air bottles coupled together and in operation when you selected 'combustor start' on the flight deck the air from the bottles would be directed directly into the engine starter motor. This was then followed by a normal start procedure. This system was very noisy and whilst effective, it was also a pain in the backside for us having to recharge the bottles, and because the start cycle had been initiated the air pressure would have been completely used. Contrary to some Internet web sites we never carried spare bottles in the freight hold.

Another tedious problem was with the cabin pressurisation system. It was engine driven by a

JOHN STUCKE @ GMAIL - COM

0117 4222061

Inland Revenue South East: An Executive Office of the Inland Revenue

Director: Tony Sleeman

Could you please drop me an email on rogercreasey@btinternet.com or phone me on 01342 833781 just to let me know you have received the book.

Many thanks Roger

Harry.

Lovely hearing from you, I am only advertising through D.T. & BCM & John in Smallfield the rest is by word of mouth. Therefore if you find the book interesting maybe you could let others know.

We are selling at £7.00 Collected out £10.75 Posted. We have only 90 copies in four ...

Rog

compressor unit fitted to the top of the Conway engine. The only part that let the system down was the flight deck indicator system that indicated cabin compressor operation. The indicator system was generated by a small brass worm gear and this was forever wearing out and therefore giving false indications. However, over time our Flight Engineers had become aware of the problem and always managed to work around it.

The VC10 was a very solid aircraft structurally, well thought out and well built. However, we did experience minor problems in what was called the 'stub plane', this being the structure between the engine and the fuselage. There was a small angle section fitted to one of the frames, which occasional cracked so we contacted Vickers, the aircraft manufacturers who told us to 'stop drill' the crack with a quarter of an inch drill, which we did. However the next time we inspected the aircraft we found it had cracked beyond the hole we had drilled and the crack was now about two inches long. Again we contacted Vickers who told us to drill it again at the end of the crack and this we did. The very next time we checked we found the crack was now about three inches long! This time I think Vickers threw the towel in by saying, "okay we don't even need the angle section so remove it completely and throw it away". The most permanent and best solution for all concerned I think.

Chapter 41

June 25th 1966 saw my fiancée Rosemary and I marry and as we had planned we flew to Rio for our honeymoon. As mentioned earlier our hotel cost us 10 shillings a night, however, when we arrived we found the price had gone up and kept going up until we were paying £3 a night! What a shock for us both just starting out, £3 was a heck of a lot of money in those days and everything else around us increased in price daily too. Inflation was running at something approaching 100 per cent.

The hotel laid on a trip to Sterns the Jewellers that was 'free'. Great we thought, however, having made the trip we found that to get back to the hotel we needed to get a taxi. With our past experiences of this place freshly in our minds all we could do was watch the taxi's meter whizzing round in fear of what the final damage might be to our finances. However, common sense prevailed in the end and as we saw the meter pass 'ridiculous' and firmly head for 'insane' so we stopped the taxi, paid ridiculous money and walked the rest of the way back to the hotel.

This trip to Rio was the first time Rosemary had ever flown in an aircraft and as we were staff we were seated right at the very back of the aircraft. This is where knowledge of aircraft construction and operation can either be good or bad! On the

VC10 the hydraulics are sited behind the aft toilets so that when the crew made demands on the system you would get weird noises coming from the hydraulics behind the toilets and this alarmed Rosemary quite a bit, I'm sure she must have thought something awful was happening to the aircraft.

The VC10 also operated up to Santiago and as luck (or bad) had it when we were leaving to come home the aircraft got stuck there in fog. It hardly seems possible these days what with credit cards etc. but the truth is that back in those days we had no financial backup, all we had was the travellers cheques and a small amount of cash, the like of which had long since disappeared under a cloud of raging inflation! With this new set of circumstances (our aircraft being delayed) we had to stay an extra couple of days with no money whatsoever. Fortunately for us however I knew the Station Engineer, Robbie Jewett and he came to our rescue by lending us some cash. Good old Robbie, he had taken us out a few times to see various places of interest during our stay. One of the things that amused us whilst travelling with Robbie and meeting some of the locals, and as people of a certain age will appreciate, 1966 was the year England won the football World Cup. We were continually being asked if we knew Bobby Charlton. The locals were crazy about football and on the Copacabana Beach it wasn't easy to find a spot to sit on that didn't have goal posts or a football pitch marked out.

In comparison our eventual flight back home, although delayed turned out to be a good laugh. As usual we were seated right at the back of the aircraft and were treated to in-flight service by a handful of Brazilians who had somehow charmed the airhostesses, took their uniform hats and put them on themselves. They proceeded to parade up and down the cabin serving drinks and meals, all very much in good humour. This was all taken in the best of spirits and upset nobody.

We paid Robbie back over a period of time by sending over to him on various aircraft tins of fruit, jam and peas, in fact anything he could not buy in Rio. I used to give a package to the Flight Crew to hand over to Robbie, so all above board no rules or regulations broken.

Quite soon after our marriage, I was asked to go to Entebbe, Uganda, as a Relief Engineer for two or three weeks just until Jack Dunkley, the permanent engineer came back from leave.

On my arrival I found that I had missed seeing Jack Dunkley for a hand-over as he was returning home on the same aircraft that I had arrived on. I managed to find his office and the note he had left for me on his desk which read something like, 'the flying programme consists of VC10s

258

and Britannias. The VC10s operate Nairobi, Lusaka and N'dola and note that you have to reduce tyre pressures to fly to Lusaka and N'dola and then re-inflate them back to normal pressure when the aircraft returns to Entebbe'.

The next item on Jack's note concerned spares. He said, "they are in the compound and the key is in the top drawer of my desk". The note went on to say "at present it rains at about 10 o'clock every morning when the Britannia arrives". Jack concluded his letter by saying, "best of luck, if all else fails you will find a bottle of scotch in the bottom drawer of the desk".

On my flight from London on the VC10, I remember that one of the passengers was refused entry into Entebbe; his only option was to be put straight back onto the aircraft and fly with it all the way around the whole route until he eventually arrived back at London.

Jack was right in his warning to me about the rain every morning, yes it did rain at about 10 o'clock and I got soaked most days. However it was very hot and as such I dried out pretty quickly. The only real danger was the mosquitoes and the need to avoid them at all costs.

There was a golf course nearby and one afternoon I decided to take a walk around it. I saw a few people on the way but not too many.

One young lad sticks in my memory though because all he had to play with was an old gnarled piece of stick with a bulbous end to it, despite his lack of clubs he managed to hit golf balls straight down the middle of the fairway and for a very good distance too. At this point all thoughts of my perhaps playing a round deserted me, as I felt quite eclipsed by his sterling efforts!

Chapter 42

When I started back at Gatwick I decided it was time that I applied to the CAA for a Type Licence on the Conway engine. I filled in the relevant paperwork including the work sheets. In due course I received a reply saying that as I had not changed a main engine driven fuel pump up to now I would not be accepted. Feeling rather deflated by this rejection but not put off by any means, I replied back to them saying that in British United, to date we had not even replaced a fuel pump. This must have made them think as the return letter stated that they would contact our local Rolls Royce Rep, Gordon Cope, and if he was agreeable he would be asked to verbally take me through all the aspects of a fuel pump change, with me answering all of his questions. He would then contact the CAA and on his say so, I would be accepted for an examination on the Conway engine. So it seemed that persistence paid off.

Subsequently Gordon and I went through all of the requirements and the CAA were satisfied and gave me a date for the examination. The interview was to be held at Heathrow, I believe it was Hut 13 near the old Eagle Hangar.

I remember it was quite daunting really; I sat in the examination room with two CAA examiners sitting opposite me. One of them must have been the local BOAC Surveyor and he gave me the impression that he thought I was "trying it on" by saying that we at BUA had not changed fuel pumps because BOAC had changed lots of them. This examination lasted well into two hours and to say I felt punch drunk at the end of this exceedingly in-depth discussion about the Conway engine as fitted to the VC10 would be a vast understatement. He must have been a very hands on type of surveyor because he was asking very detailed and specific questions such as "which fasteners do you release first to open the cowlings" I think he was finally convinced in the end because he realised that if I had not played around with the engine attachment to the airframe, called the 'swinging link', I could not have answered his questions. As I said goodbye, got in my car to drive home, I think my brain was so scrambled that I managed to pick up the wrong road coming out of the Airport and finished up in the centre of London, I had to come home via Brixton but nevertheless I was glad it was over, the difficult part was now to wait for the results, fortunately I passed.

Ever wishing to advance my knowledge and skills it was some time later that I applied to sit for a licence on the Rolls Royce Spey fitted to the BAC 1-11. This time the examination venue was slightly more local being at CAA Headquarters in Redhill, Surrey.

I arrived there early and sat in the waiting room. Whilst waiting to be called in for the interview, I think I must have had a touch of examination nerves, as I couldn't remember how many stages of compressor were fitted to the Spey, a basic piece of knowledge. Whilst having a mental panic, I picked up a Flight International magazine, which was on the table near to my seat, and low and behold there was a centrefold page showing a cut away section of the Spey engine! My goodness I thought, someone must have been looking after me that day.

The examiner on this engine did something rather similar to what I had experienced before. Taking a piece of blank paper he drew a straight line with a pen, handing it to me he said "that is the front of the nose cowling, now draw the engine".

Having successfully obtained Type Licences on both the Conway and Spey engines together with a Viscount Airframe Licence and Dart engine gained some years previous, I considered it was time to call a halt to further applications for Type Licences. My reasoning here was:

a) The financial gain was not worth the hassle you received 15 shillings for the first licence, 10 shillings for the next and finally 5 shillings for any additional.

b) The other reason being I recognised that times were changing and the word on the street had it that Type Licences would soon cease to exist once larger aircraft such as the Boeing 747 came on stream. It was likely that Approved Engineers would then certify everything. This change was some way away at this time but it was how things were surely going.

Chapter 43

By this time 1965/66 we had built another bay to Hangar 3, this allowed us to get a VC10 in one end and a Britannia in the other. We took the opportunity of this new build to try to resolve some issues we had with Hangar 3. The main problem was that following a prolonged heavy downpour of rain, water somehow managed to seep into the various pits that were built into the hangar floor. These pits contained hoses and adaptors, which were connected to a large compressor situated in the corner of the hangar. The compressor supplied air pressure to underground pipes that terminated in these pits. The air lines were used for various purposes for example one was used to jack up the aircraft, another operated pneumatic drills and rivet guns, therefore when the rain filled the pits with water it penetrated the various hoses and as a consequence when the engineer attempted to operate a drill or anything else air driven water came out of the end of it. We never did find a way to fix this problem so eventually the pits were concreted over and we ran pneumatic air hoses above ground across the hangar floor.

Another slightly embarrassing thing about the hangar was that when we had a Britannia in the west end of it for servicing invariably the aircraft would be jacked up to make retraction checks of the undercarriage. However, when the aircraft

265

was lowered back down the nose wheels would most likely not be in exactly the same position as when the aircraft was towed into the hangar. Bearing in mind the length of the aircraft fuselage, the problem here was that as we hooked up the tractor to tow it out of the hangar, we invariably managed to get the tail plane stuck behind some of the girder structure of the hangar roof support. It would then take upwards to half an hour, gradually shunting the aircraft back and forward until it cleared the structure. 'Sods Law' meant that this usually happened on a Friday night when everybody had had enough and just wanted to get away home.

Over the years we had a few problems with the VC10. At one point in time we removed and refitted quite a few of the Conway 540 engines. Eventually of course we actually ran out of spare engines and had to obtain permission from the CAA to use a spare engine that was at the Vickers site in Weybridge that was used on the prototype VC10. This engine was not certified for commercial operation so we had to have a special dispensation from the CAA to use it. When the engine arrived it had many cable looms that were used for test purposes. These looms had to be capped and stowed. When the engine arrived from Vickers to Gatwick a chap called Bill Buss arrived with it. Bill eventually got a job with British United and so joined our Project & Development Department.

We had one not so memorable week when one of the VC10s G-ASIW was taken out of service and put in the hangar to be really smartened up and when finished it would be used for a royal flight. The aircraft spent the whole week in the hangar and on its last night the chap in charge of the night shift decided it would be easier to jack the aircraft up to replace the main wheels. The only problem was when he lowered the aircraft back down to the ground the tail jack slipped out of position and damaged the fuselage and tail plane. Fortunately for us we had a standby aircraft and this had to be prepared at very short notice.

My wife Rosemary remembers this particular fiasco very well, with all its resultant interviews of staff whereby she took days and days of shorthand notes compiling the report, filling shorthand notebooks by the dozen and then having to type it all back.

On completion of the repairs Brian Trubshaw, the chief test pilot of Vickers Armstrong latterly of Concorde fame, carried out the subsequent Flight Test

VC10 Tail removal

Hole in the fuselage where the tail jack finished up

G-ASIW in the hangar with the nose jacked up

We were very fortunate after this incident to have two Inspectors from Vickers to work with us; one of which was Bill Fagan and the other Buster Pickard. Both were very experienced structural engineers. After working alongside us for some time they each left Vickers and took up full time employment with us.

On or about 1966/67 we introduced a new system into the Engineering Department and this was called 'Quality Control'. This meant that some of our Inspectors were promoted from their present roles to become Quality Control Engineers. As a result of these changes some of our staff that up until now had been classified as Chargehands, and this included me, were promoted to the job title of "Check Supervisors", the equivalent of the "Assistant Foreman" rank. The effect of this new job role meant that we were given the responsibility of care of an aircraft whilst it was in the hangar for maintenance.

Also at this time we set up our own Engineering Training School. Eddie Dove who had been a Deputy Chief Inspector headed this up. Incidentally it was Eddie who first took me on as an Aircraft Inspector way back in 1961. Two Airframe Instructors who came from BAC ably assisted him. In fact these two instructors had been our original instructors on the BAC 1-11 and VC10, a small world. Among our numbers there was also a chap called Dave Campbell who prior to joining our team was a Royce Rolls

Representative, he became our 'Engine Instructor'. He turned out to be a very good choice. Pete Horsecroft who had been an Electrical Inspector became an Instructor on Avionics.

So it was then that by the time we ordered the BAC 1-11 500 series aircraft in 1968, for delivery in 1969, we already had our own training set up in place together with our own instructors. It was at this time that once we had finished the course we sat our final examination paper, if we passed we were then able to apply to the Quality Control Department for further examination and provided they were happy, we were approved to work on the aircraft. The foregoing procedure initially seemed rather 'cock-eyed' because it meant that we would be sitting the same course as the Quality Control guy who would subsequently examine us!

The 500 series 1-11 had a longer fuselage than the 200 series and was therefore better balanced on the ground so there was no need for the ballast we normally had in the forward hold whilst towing the aircraft. The Spey 512 engines were much more powerful and all round it was a much-improved aircraft.

With the introduction of Quality Control we no longer had the local CAA Surveyor conducting hangar visits; it was now for the Quality

Department to carry out their own survey. It was all quite difficult to start with because the Quality Department would also have their own inspection requirements on the aircraft. For instance, one of our Inspectors would carry out an inspection on an engine raising his own set of defects followed by the Quality guy doing his survey and of course coming up with his defects. This caused some confusion on occasions as it could happen that the Hangar Inspector would say, "that part is okay" only to find the Quality guy had said, "no I want it changed". As I said, it could get a little tense at times.

It took a little while to settle into a more stable routine and then it became a real asset. With the likes of Sid Finch and Ron Thaxter both now Quality Control Engineers on the 1-11 aircraft. Both of them had been on the 1-11 series 200 aircraft since they were introduced into BUA service so with their vast knowledge of the aircraft they guided some of the younger qualified engineers into what was right and what was wrong.

The end of the 1960s was not a very happy time as the Airline was struggling to make money and after I left work one evening and was watching the 6 o'clock news at home, I found out that a reporter was speculating about BOAC taking us over. Shortly afterwards the telephone rang and I was told to go back into work to attend a meeting in the hangar for all the staff, this meeting was arranged by the Chief Engineer who was to tell us what was going on. It turned out that he didn't know much about it himself. Anyway, eventually it all blew over and we carried on as before. However, the latter part of 1969 saw the writing on the wall so far as British United was concerned.

Chapter 44

But before we close the hangar doors finally on British United Airways I want to add some stories about a few people.

Arnold Sheead and Bill Richardson

Arnold, coming from Yorkshire as he did, had a saying, which he used when he wanted to tell you something that was to be kept quiet, he would say. "Hey lad, between you me and gate post".

Arnold's office at one time was always left unlocked and a couple of our lads used to take a look around it when they were on night shift to see if there was anything of interest (knowledge is power). Somehow, we were never quite sure how, Arnold realised this was happening so he set a trap. One night he left a box on his desk, which vaguely resembled a jack-in-a-box size knowing that curiosity would get the better of his twilight snoopers. Of course that night as the snoop patrol got under way in Arnold's office, seeing the box, as predicted, temptation was far too great and the box began to be opened but as soon as it was touched a whole load of paper and playing cards shot out of it covering the desk. Desperate efforts then ensued, stuffing, pushing and shoving, all to no avail, as all this debris was virtually impossible to repatriate inside the box! Eventually, conceding defeat at the clear-up operation it was left in position and no further attempt was made to disguise the evidence. Suffice it to say that was the last snoop patrol of the office.

In my view Bill Richardson and Arnold were the driving force behind British United's successful engineering department. Bill was a very quiet sort of person but he was the technical brain. Arnold was very much the force in getting things done. He was also extremely loyal and protective of his staff. I remember on one occasion when he was Chief Inspector, he defended one of his Inspectors over some infringement in front of the production staff. However later, in the privacy of his office, he told his Inspector off good and proper for causing the problem in the first place.

Arnold didn't like his Inspectors sitting down in their office when everyone else was working on the aircraft, so when Hangar 3 was first built one of the offices at the back of the hangar was for the inspection staff, however he instructed the builders not to put any chairs in the office he said "If they want a chair they can go and find one"

John Titterall

John Titterall was the other tea boy at Croydon. John spent his whole career, like me, with Transair, BUA, BCAL and BA. He told me a year or so ago that his most favourite time was the BUA years. John now spends a very happy retirement in the West Country.

I asked John if he would like to make any comments regarding his career and his recollections follow: -

When he first started as a boy at Croydon (a year or so before me) some ground rules had to be set, he was told that 'cleanliness is next to godliness' when it comes to working on aircraft. Like me, he was also told never to call it a PLANE it's an AEROPLANE. Jim Marks and Pete Peters took John to a shop in Croydon to buy some tools just to get him started (people used to look after you in those days).

One of his recollections was when a Morton Airways DH Dove, flown by Ben Gunn, could not get the undercarriage down on landing, so he had to do a wheels-up landing. That was quite a sight and slightly terrifying not knowing what would happen.

He also remembered the day he saw Wally with his overalls on fire. He said that has been a lasting memory for him.

John worked with two fitters, Jim Marks and Buck Taylor (the other boys, including me were so envious, we all wanted to work with those two). John said anytime he made a mistake or

276

did anything wrong he had to buy sweets for Jim and Buck as a punishment…. "Good old days".

Jim Hughes

I was starting early morning shift when my boss said we have a new Supervisor starting today he has come from BOAC so he is going to find our working practices a lot different to what he's been used to. Pete said, "The new guy has a Conway licence so get him to shadow you all day". Pete introduced me to one of the nicest people you could ever wish to know, his name was Jim Hughes and he was in his mid 20s. I took Jim outside and told him we have a VC10 to do some engine runs on, the time was about 06:15 and by 06:45 we were in a BAC 1-11 running the engines, out of that and straight into a Bristol Britannia followed by one of the DC6 aircraft. I told Jim we had one more job to do that was to taxi the Cessna 310 down to the ramp then it would be about 08:00 and time for breakfast. Jim was a bit shell-shocked and said "is it always like this?" I said most morning's follow this pattern, he said he would be lucky to do much at all before breakfast.

Stan Sackett

About 1964, an Engine Fitter joined our shift; he came from the Royal Navy and then BEA. His name was Stan Sackett. Stan found it difficult to settle in to start with as he was quite set in his ways and we were not always the most organised bunch. It's funny the turns that life takes because I never hit it off straight away with Stan.

My wife Rosemary left BUA in 1967 to give birth to our first daughter. She then got a part time job in 1969 in a company called Gate Engraving just down the bottom of our road in Crawley. She came home one night and said the lady I work with is so nice I have invited her and her husband round to see us. Yes, her name was Joan Sackett and Stan was her husband. For whatever reason, out of work Stan and I got on fine and have remained friends ever since.

In 1970 they emigrated to South Africa with their three children and still live there now. They lived in Johannesburg for a few years and then moved down to Durban with South African Airways who Stan worked for until he retired.

Most years we would visit them around the end of June, although it was their winter and nights were a bit chilly, daytime was very warm for us. Also Joan and Stan and Our Wedding Anniversary are on the same day, 25th June. They celebrated their 60th in 2015 and we celebrated our 50th in 2016.

When they came to us we would have holidays in England or we would meet sometimes in America and have vacations over there together. Over the years we have had so many enjoyable holidays together. To this day we still keep in touch albeit with letters in cards at Christmas time and Birthdays.

Bert Smith

Bert Smith was our Maintenance Electrician at Gatwick. He told me a story about the roof on Hangar 1. One day he was working on some electrical installation on the roof of the hangar when he noticed that the material the roof had been manufactured from had started to sprout new growth. On making enquiries he found out the roof was made of compressed straw. The cause of the new crop was due to the long periods of rain we had had, the material absorbed the moisture and started to revert back to nature.

Nazie El Masry

I can't remember exactly which course I was on; it was well before smoking was banned indoors so quite a few years ago. One of our engineers El Masry, loved to smoke his pipe, it made a terrible smell. Mas, as we knew him, went out of the classroom for a toilet break. We, in the meantime, took the tobacco out of his pipe and filled it with bits of pencil eraser adding a small amount of tobacco back on top just so he wouldn't suspect. Eventually Mas came back into the classroom, stuck his pipe in his mouth and lit up. To our amazement he carried on regardless! We on the other hand sat there coughing our hearts out as he just laughed.

There are 4 engineers that I have not said much about but they all go way back with me, the first one.

Jim Williams. Jim has been around almost as long as me. He joined Transair at Croydon Airport in 1957 aged 16yrs and still lives in Horley. When we were both young lads we used to go to the cinema in Horley and if you were lucky you saw the same film all week. Jim used to be in the hangars but spent most of his time on the ramp on departures. Jim remained a tradesman and a very well respected Union Shop Steward for the AEU. He has helped out on this book at times when my memory has hit a brick wall.

John Layton. John started with us as a young lad and went on to become a qualified supervisor but eventually left us. It's unfortunate but over time you lose track of people and you only seem to meet up at funerals, this happened in John's case. I believe he is still involved with aircraft at Biggin Hill and he is the Quality Manager for Spitfire rebuilds.

Bob Cooper. Bob is very well known and worked for a lot of airlines, he is renowned for his photography and currently looks after the VC10 at Dunsfold a lasting memory of Bob for me is that of one evening getting a phone call

280

from him saying we can't start the APU on the VC10 can you remember how it all works, this was about 3 years ago and some 44 years since I last worked on one. We spent the rest of the evening phoning each other

Last but not least:

Ian Bagshaw. Once again we go way back and over the years our paths have crossed and re crossed. He is a very well respected qualified engineer, once again Ian has done everything, Hangar work, Ramp work, Outstations and Management and what I understand did not want to work for BA. I believe Ian now lives in New Zealand.

Within British United Airways and later British Caledonian we had very friendly and family orientated airlines with some engineers having either a son or a daughter working through an engineering apprenticeship, we even had two Captains with sons as engineering apprentices.

We would involve other departments like Purchasing, Flight Deck and Cabin Crew in our engineering work.

We would get in touch with the Cabin Crew office and would ask if they would like to send someone down to inspect the cabin of an aircraft that had just completed a major maintenance refit to see if we had any of the cabin equipment either missing or incorrectly stowed. This could prevent an embarrassing delay on its first commercial flight.

In the days when we had Flight Engineers they would often wander around the hangars looking at what we were doing and asking if we had any major modifications being embodied that they should know about.

We would also get to know Captains and First Officers, this could be quite handy if you were flying somewhere on holiday and they would invite you up to the flight deck, this is a great experience for very young children, sadly this abruptly stopped with terrorism.

Favourite memory of the VC10

The VC10 suffered a lot of cracks around the engine air intakes and Vickers, the manufacturers, arranged for each aircraft in turn to have modifications carried out at Wisley airfield. Each aircraft was at Wisley for about 2 weeks while the modifications were made. The opportunity was taken for other planned work to be done on each aircraft at the same time as the modification programme and this involved our own working party travelling each day from Gatwick to Wisley. In order to get the aircraft into the hangar we had to remove the wing tips and to facilitate the air intake modifications we needed to remove all 4 engines.

On completion of the entire work programme engine ground run testing was carried out and a test flight was needed before return to revenue service.

It was in the middle of winter when the last aircraft to have this work carried out was due to happen. Soon the day arrived to do the engine ground testing; to start with we struggled getting it out of the hangar with snow laying on the ground. Once out of the hangar the wing tips were re-fitted. It was usual to position the aircraft on a bit of a slope near the hangar prior to carrying out the engine tests. However, on this occasion it was too slippery to carry out high power engine checks so with the agreement of the flight crew who were going to carry out the air test and fly the aircraft back to Gatwick, it was decided we would do all the relevant low power checks and then check for any leaks, top up the engine oil levels and close all the cowlings ready for flight.

At 16:45 with the Captain and First Officer in their front seats ready for flight we taxied up onto the runway where it had been agreed all the full power runs would be carried out. Arthur Lacey and I did the entire engine checks, cleared the paperwork and threw it out of the front passenger door to Harry Leggett the engineer on the ground. What I need to say now is that we were given permission by Wisley Airport Control to do all this but the stipulation was that we must be airborne by 17:00 when the runway lights would go out. Arthur and I got out of the way to enable the Flight Engineer to get into his seat. We were rolling down the runway at 17:00 exactly, just as we lifted off the runway lights extinguished; the test flight was accomplished on route to Gatwick. The aircraft was back in service that same evening at 20:00. This was an end to a very interesting and exciting day.

One more story before we move on

At the end of 1968 Morton Air Service moved out of their Hangar into the wooden hangar and then became part of British United Island Airways (BUIA). Their old hangar was subsequently converted into BUA's Workshops. Morton's then sold off their Dove and Heron Aircraft and took over some of BUA's DC3 aircraft. When BUIA was first formed some of the Jersey Airlines engineering apprentices joined us in Hangar 1 working on the DC3 and Viscount aircraft. One of the lads was a surfing champion that is on the water kind not the Internet!

One aircraft I have forgotten to mention is the old Avro Anson parked outside Hangar 3. This was used as a trainer solely for the benefit of our apprentices. I used to take a couple of apprentices at a time and show them how to start the engines. The Avro Anson didn't stay around very long.

The old wooden hangar had seen a few changes over the years. It started off with Overseas Aviation in early 1960. BUA then used it for a while then Morton's moved in but eventually one night in the 1990's it burnt down, nobody was hurt and no equipment damaged as at that time it was only used as a storage unit

PART 3

Gatwick Airport
Years 1970-1988

British Caledonian

Chapter 45

1970 saw another new start with the formation of British Caledonian; albeit known as Caledonian//BUA until November 1971. When the Caledonian Engineering department merged with BUA Engineering it followed the usual pattern of mergers, some people felt hurt by it, others felt good about it and I guess there will always be winners and losers in such matters.

My very first introduction to Caledonian staff was when a chap walked up to me in Hangar 3 and introduced himself as Piers Deleigh. Piers and I have got on well over the years and I still see him to this day, once a month at the Aviation Meeting in Smallfield.

Piers is a brilliant Engineer, even in retirement he turns his hands to renovating old cars, and he even built his own micro-light aircraft from a kit. Piers learnt to fly the micro-light and eventually became an instructor, quite an achievement. He gave a talk about all the ups and downs, ins and outs of building and flying a micro-light and even about his forced landing.

Once the initial in-fighting of the merger had sorted itself out tranquillity such as it was returned. I must say, the two groups of staff in the hangars got on well together. Caledonian had some really good Engineers among them, Taff Jones, Ian Barber, Mike Gardener and a chap who eventually became my boss Ron Gunner.

Ron was ex Royal Air Force and had been a Japanese Prisoner of War. I believe he was in a Catalina Flying Boat that was forced down somewhere around Singapore. Ron very rarely spoke about his experiences in captivity save for on a very few occasions. On leaving the RAF he joined British Eagle which eventually folded and he then joined Caledonian along with a couple of other guys from British Eagle.

Along with the BUA fleet we now had additional BAC 1-11 500 Series aircraft, Bristol Britannia's and the Boeing 707 320C.

The aircraft were all painted in the new BCAL livery, for some of the BUA aircraft this was their third colour scheme change.

We soon started to get the B707 aircraft into the hangar for service checks. We had a mixed bag of 707s, as they were nearly all second-hand leased aircraft.

One of them, G-AXRS had to go to the U.S.A. for a period of time each year, this had something to do with the leasing agreement, and anyway this was always used for a crew training exercise as we had no simulators.

First impressions for me of a 707 was one of a rugged structure but very flexible. The four Pratt & Whitney engines slung on pylons forward of the wings were quite different to what we had been working on.

We now adopted a shift pattern, which gave us a permanent Foreman on night shift namely Charlie Hilton. The lads on the shop floor rotated shifts onto nights about every three or four weeks and we as check supervisors were doing nights every four weeks.

At about this time we had two or three Supervisors who were employed to procure third party work. We started to get private BAC 1-11 aircraft that belonged to various Arab Sheiks. One or two of these aircraft I remember well. One of them was painted in the hangar and after finding out that the flag on the tail was upside down, which was very quickly rectified, then the aircraft was completed and was due for delivery to the Sheiks daughter for her 18th Birthday. The second I recall was fitted with white carpets inside at a cost, at that time, well over £300 per sq. metre. We had to lay carpet runners on the floor; these were lengths of plastic that you walked on. Engineers or anybody who worked on the aircraft had to wear white over shoes, white gloves and disposable paper overalls. The interior of the aircraft was fitted out with armchairs and a double bed. The bathroom taps and toilet fittings were in gold plate. The seats by the way were all made of leather.

Pete Buckland, one of our Engineers was contracted to one of these private aircraft and he told us some stories. One he related was when he walked around the aircraft at Saudi or one of those states, I can't remember which, a courier arrived and said, "get the aircraft ready, the crew will be arriving shortly and they are going to fly somewhere or other to deliver a letter for the Sheik". Another story he told us was when on a trip to Los Angeles, he was told by the Agent they were now on 'stand down' and it was okay for them to leave the airport but not go anywhere that would take them more than 30 minutes to get back. It's a different world.

Another job the guys on the Third Party Team were trying to get for us was regarding a Boeing 747 freighter belonging to Flying Tigers, an American outfit. This aircraft had suffered from over rotation on take-off and had scraped the underside of the aft fuselage. Dave Lear (ex-apprentice) now a qualified supervisor and myself went to inspect the damage. The repair was not to be carried out straight away; Flying Tigers initially just wanted us to quote for the repair. Dave and I came up with a rough idea of how many man-hours it would take to repair the aircraft and submitted our report to the engineering department. However, by the time our report had gone through the various stages of the engineering chain of command we had managed to price ourselves out of the job as everybody had added their own ten percent to the quote.

By this time we were getting more experience with the Boeing 707 aircraft and we found that the Pratt & Whitney JT3D engines were very robust but touchy if you ran an engine at high power with anything like a tail wind or a cross wind. Under these circumstances you could get an engine surge, which would result in a very large bang followed by flames coming out of the air intake. To our surprise the engines were so robust they just carried on working normally.

The 1970s saw us taking on major maintenance on the 707s where they would be in our hangar for anything up to 6 weeks at a time. We would use approximately 30,000 man-hours to achieve the workload.

One problem we found with the 707 was that it suffered from corrosion. One 707 which happened to be one of the freighter aircraft, on strip down, we found that the sound proofing bags in the crown area of the fuselage were soaking wet with water. On further inspection we needed to undertake more than a hundred repairs to the roof structure.

Another 707 had had a mercury spillage in the forward freight hold and this was so bad that we had to get a team over from Boeing to carry out the repairs. When the working party arrived we found they had brought everything they could possibly need, in addition to tooling and equipment they even brought their own toilet rolls! This group were known as the Specialist AOG Team.

Whilst the aircraft was with us a major inspection was carried out. During the inspection we jacked it up off the ground and correctly supported it. The American guys then got to work on it. They removed in excess of 20 feet of the lower fuselage an equivalent to the whole lower forward freight hold. They then returned to their factory in America and manufactured a replacement section. Whilst the AOG Team were away it was my job upon arrival in the hangar each morning to sight along the top of the fuselage to make certain there were no wrinkles appearing anywhere along its length.

After a few weeks the team arrived back with the new fuselage section and set about drilling and riveting it back together. They worked very fast and hard, and I noticed one guy holding a windy drill in each of his hands drilling off holes, he resembled a cowboy of the 'wild west' firing off both six guns at his target.

The B707 major check was quite something to see, we had to remove all 4 engines and disconnect the pylons supporting the engines. Once disconnected the pylons would sit on special stands that we had manufactured specifically for this purpose. We then proceeded to remove the fin and rudder, elevators and tail planes. At this stage the aircraft would be jacked up and the undercarriages would be removed. The next process was to strip the cabin down to bare metal; this was followed by the flying controls associated with the wings.

The first aircraft we stripped down in this way caused us much difficulty in removing the wing leading edge fittings. The Boeing representative who was observing us during this inspection saw our difficulty and to our surprise said "you boys want to use a hammer", we didn't need much encouragement to get the hammer out so quickly one of our lads grabbed a hide faced mallet out of his tool box to which the Boeing guy Sam said "no get a **hammer**". Sam went off to Stores and came back with a rather large club hammer; the Boeing guy said right "now hit it with that", when low and behold the leading edge fittings all fell apart with no further damage. Sam said the 707 were like a Ford tractor, very robust and won't let you down. Another 'learning curve' they were never ending at this stage in aviation development.

All the Boeing 707 major maintenance inputs included an incredible amount of Boeing service bulletins. These service bulletins were basically life improvement modifications. Most of the work was carried out on the wings; we had to replace a lot of what was called Hi loc fasteners. These fasteners were roughly speaking a cross between a rivet and a nut and bolt. The fuel tanks had to be drained as a lot of the work was carried out inside the wing tanks. Later on we had mods to carry out on the horizontal stabiliser centre torque box. Most of these mods involved some form of shift work to get the aircraft finished on schedule. All these years later I still remember some of the Service Bulletin numbers e.g. BSB2510 Top Wing Skin Rework, BSB2957 Wing Rear Spar Rework, BSB2496 and 2492 Lower Wing Skin Rework and so on.

The aircraft would also undergo a complete paint job whilst in the hangar. I had about 130 engineers working on these major checks and at the same time sanding discs would be rubbing down the paintwork. When the bodywork was ready to be repainted the lads would go to lunch at 12:00 while the painters started to re-spray the aircraft. During this procedure the hangar would be shrouded in a fine paint spray dust cloud. The painters would finish spraying at about 12:40 but nobody would go near the aircraft until the hangar foreman Fred Ansell had walked from his office out into the hangar, looked around and sniffed the air, if he was satisfied there was no spray fumes left he would say "ok everyone back to work." We would be back at work on the aircraft by 13:00 having lost only about 30 minutes.

Working on the B707 in Hangar 3 was basically a continuous workload and whilst we were completing one aircraft we would be planning the next one. That detailed planning usually fell to Eric Ludkin, John Stuckle, and myself. The specific responsibilities were split such that Eric looked after the avionic side, John controlled the planning aspects of the job while I looked after the engine and airframe together with Mike Gardener and we were later joined by Ian Barber who oversaw the whole project. Later on Mike and Ian moved on and we reported directly to Ron Gunner.

BCAL, unbeknown to any of us on the shop floor, acquired three B707 aircraft from Qantas. Upon arrival all three aircraft needed a major maintenance input plus a repaint job into BCAL colours.

We acquired one other B707, which came into our hangar via Stanstead where it had been parked for some time. It was in a dreadful state but fortunately for us we had some excellent engineers at that time, some of whom come to mind, Buster Pickard, Bill Fagan, Wilf Tobell,

George Thomas, Dave Jenner, Miles Davis, Stan Nelhams and the ever faithful Bom Debansi, these were the mainstay of supervisors. For fitters we had the likes of Dave Lear, Pete Hollingsworth, John Mitchell, Geoff Lewis, Noel Peazold, Jim Hook, Gus Ford, Len Bean, Harry Leggett and Tony Harper.

In the early 1970's the company went through a series of redundancies due to financial pressures, which affected those working in the hangar badly. As a result we lost some very good people, the redundancies were, as is usual, based on the principal of last in and first out.

Following this period of depressing redundancies things settled down again the engineering management began to take on anyone who wanted to come back, and to safe guard ourselves for the future we used contract labour from a recognised source to fill any shortages of staff. This worked well in one way because it allowed us to be flexible with regards to staffing levels i.e. Get rid of contractors when we wanted to, conversely however they had no allegiance to us and if they found a better paying contract they would up sticks and go no matter what job they were doing. False economy I'm not sure?

As said previously BUA had operated 4 VC10 aircraft. G-ARTA was written off after a landing accident in January 1972. The other 3 operated until 1973/4 when they became more or less redundant due to the increasing number of B707 aircraft in the fleet and lack of engineering support around the routes. We all felt very sorry to see them go. G-ARTA had a sad end. The BCAL website covers the accident in fine detail, what I will say is that Dave Record and a team of engineers from the Ramp recovered the aircraft from the runway, in David's words the recovery was not simple due to two factors, one being the nose landing gear damage and the other being once they coupled up a tractor and started to tow the aircraft they found it would not follow in a straight line due to the damaged fuselage.

With the aircraft finally in Hangar 3 a structures engineer from Vickers at Weybridge inspected it and apart from joking that if we jacked the aircraft up then dropped it maybe we could straighten the fuselage. The Boeing rep we had old Sam looked at the aircraft and said if this had happened in the USA we would have the aircraft mounted some place as a roadside café.

So that was the end of a very beautiful aircraft she was towed carefully out of the hangar and parked behind the blast bank between hangar 3 and the wooden hangar and after a period of time broken up. Some people took small parts as souvenirs.

*G-ARTA in the run pen at LGW you can see
the blast bank behind the aircraft and behind
that was the wooden hangar where we
deposited a set of steps one night blown there
by the engines.*

*G-ARTA after the accident the
aircraft eventually got broken
up for scrap tragic end for a
lovely aircraft.*

We had a contract with Middle East Airlines (MEA.) to service their VC10. On one occasion I was on night shift as Check Controller (i.e. in charge of night shift). As I arrived at Hangar 3 I noticed more cars than usual parked in the car park and just thought there must be a lot of overtime being worked.

As the night shift staff started to assemble around the aircraft and we had figured out the night shift priorities one of the lads said I have just seen someone looking over from the top floor of the hangar 3-crew room. The crew room was built in the corner of the hangar and had 3 floors, the ground floor was the toilets, second floor was the crew and locker room, and the top floor was an open storage area.

A couple of us went up the stairs to investigate and found a number of Police, Drug Squad and Custom Officers up there. They told us they were on the look out for any stranger coming into the hangar. Apparently during the dayshift one of the guys had found a package of drugs hidden behind one of the aircrafts rear toilets and obviously it had been reported to the authorities.

Once the night shift lads heard what was going on, well the police etc. called it a night and left the hangar because the lads were calling out to them the likes of "we know what you are doing, and not seen anyone yet!"

Chapter 46

(The Malawi Adventure)

October 1974 saw us with a VC10, which was sold to Air Malawi. We carried out the necessary maintenance in the hangar and then re-sprayed it into Air Malawi's colour scheme.

There was a requirement for 4 Engineers to be seconded to Air Malawi for six months. These comprised 3 Engineers with recent ramp maintenance experience and one with hangar operation experience. Robbie Jewett, Dave Record and the late Trevor Adams came from the ramp area and I was the fourth to go with hangar operation experience. We were also allowed to take our families with us.

This contract also called for BCAL flight deck and cabin crew to accompany the aircraft in order to complete the crew training in Malawi.

So in December 1974 we flew with the aircraft to Malawi where on arrival we were met by a small number of Air Malawi staff. I must admit at this time none of us knew much about the country or their operation, this was about to change very quickly.

Malawi is situated in Central Africa with many mountains fairly close to the Airport; at that time the Airport itself was situated at Chileka, which was approximately an hour's drive from the town of Blantyre. The Airport was quite small and very picturesque.

Initially our whole team and their wives stayed in the Ryalls Hotel in the centre of the town of Blantyre, which stood on a 'one up' and 'one down' main road with a few smaller roads leading off it. However, as time went on Dave and his family together with my family moved into a very large bungalow. Dave and family were at one end and we were at the other.

Malawi itself was a very picturesque country; all the local Malawians were very friendly provided you observed their dress code and general practices. There was, however, a few rules that had to be observed in Malawi such as the ladies were not allowed to show their knees so had to wear long skirts. The men could not wear bell-bottom trousers, which were fashionable in the UK at that time, nor could they have long hair. Robbie's two boys were not allowed into the country until their hair was cut which Robbie promptly did with a pair of scissors in the Custom's Hall. Some newspapers and magazines were banned and certain pictures and adverts were blanked out.

The story behind this secondment was that there had been an aircraft crash whilst carrying Malawian gold miners so the Malawian Government decided they wanted all the gold miners out of South Africa.

We found out the day after our arrival that the VC10 we were to look after was going to be used to fly to Johannesburg in South Africa. It would fly out empty and then pick up a full load of 144 Malawian miners each time. Initially we did three trips a day, giving us basically an 18 hr day.

So, our first job was to reconfigure the aircraft to 144 seats then we put black plastic seat covers over the existing seat covers.

Trevor Adams, engineer from the ramp area didn't arrive for the first few weeks of the job so it was left to the 3 of us to work together each day to get the aircraft settled into the operation. Initially the VC10 flew three times a day to Jo'burg and back a trip of approximately 2 hours each way with an hour on the ground. The first flight would start at 06:00 and the last one would arrive back to the airport at around 23:00. It was necessary for one of us to fly with the aircraft on each trip and all three of us finished up with upset stomach mostly due to the heat, water, ice, etc. We hadn't initially realised that these types of flights would continue for the whole 6 months, either using the VC10 or their own BAC 1-11 400 series aircraft.

Once Trevor arrived we were summoned to see the Chief Engineer who asked for our Inspection Approval Books so that he could send them off to the local CAA Office to get them validated for Malawi. He then told us that for the rest of the contract we would split into shifts and basically take over the ramp operation whilst his staff, were away for training. This left only one ex (I believe he was retired) BOAC employee on the ramp at that point in time. I worked with Trevor, whilst Dave and Robbie worked together. We had half a dozen local Malawians on each shift who were cleaners/maintenance workers who did anything and everything.

One prominent memory was that the Chief Engineer gave us two white Ford Zephyr cars to use so when it rained and we went along the dirt roads they very quickly turned a paler shade of mud!

Our early shift started at 06:00 which meant getting up, at the latest, by 04:30 thereby leaving a good hour to get to the Airport which was advisable as you never knew what you would meet on the road. It was a little scary at times at that time of the morning finding broken down lorries and people wandering around.

The operation was so short staffed it was necessary for us to double up to help out. Air Malawi had a hangar with day shift staff working on a service check but once again not many people.

In 1974 the Airline had the VC10, two BAC 1-11 400 aircraft that had wide tyres, two Viscounts two Avro 748 and two Britten Norman Islander.

When our Inspection Approval Books returned from the local CAA we found we had been given coverage on all the Air Malawi fleet plus all other aircraft arriving at the Airport needing assistance.

On top of all other commitments we still had to cover the trips to Jo' Burg, sometimes on the VC10 and at others on the BAC 1-11. We arranged it such that the guy off duty would cover the trips to Jo' Burg. All in all it was quite a gruelling schedule especially when Air Malawi Operations decided to carry out crew training on the 1-11s in between flying normal scheduled service.

To some ears this crew training might not seem to amount to very much so far as we were involved but just to enlighten, it required that the aircraft be jacked up on the ramp, all main wheels being removed and refitted with standard tyres, the reason for this being a shortage of 'wide' tyres. Once the crew training was finished the whole process had to be repeated in reverse, replacing standard with 'wide' tyres. All this while still carrying on with schedule flying

Other services carried out at this time were flights to Seychelles, Mauritius and a schedule flight to Jo' Burg. The Airline also took on ad hoc charters. One weekend I was fortunate enough to go to Salisbury, Rhodesia, on to Dar es Salaam and Nairobi and finally back to Blantyre. As you can imagine I saw a fair bit of East Africa that weekend.

The flight deck crews were a mixed bunch of South African, Rhodesian and English nationals.

The Air Rhodesia Viscounts that would operate through Malawi were not allowed to let their cabin crew get off the aircraft because they all wore mini-skirts.

In some ways flying in Malawi reminded me of a sort of International Bush Airfield.

The whole 6 months was hard work but a lot of fun. The crews were very friendly and easy to get on with, the maintenance workers were local Malawians some of whom lived up to 5 miles away from the Airport and they used to walk to work and still had to be in by 06:00 for early shift. One morning Trevor and I were completely alone, no one else had turned up which left just the two of us to depart both of the 1-11s ourselves. When the lads did all finally turn up much, much later and we asked what had happened, they said the hyenas had got into the village and they had to walk another two to three miles in order to get to work, the worst that could happen back home would either be the bus being late or the wrong kind of leaves being on the rail track!

During our time in Malawi we had some nice trips out sightseeing in the countryside. However, I do recall on one occasion when our whole team were out together and having driven over some dried up river beds followed by a walk into the bush in an effort to find Livingstone Falls which we never found, it was very hot so Dave's wife Karen and my wife Rosemary tucked their long skirts into their waist bands and we continued our quest but after a very long walk in the heat and not finding the Falls we decided to give up on it and return to the cars. By this time we were all very thirsty and said we would get to the first Village and get some drinks. On arrival in the Village we piled out of the cars and were confronted by the local Head Guy who noticed that Rosemary had not let her skirt back down, and Karen's two boys he deemed were wearing too wide trouser legs, so to our horror he arrested them! Robbie came to the rescue though by pleading with the guy saying everybody was very sorry and that we were in the Country to service the President's aeroplane. On hearing this he eventually relented and let us all go. Just shows how easy it is to get into trouble without even trying.

All in all Malawi was a great experience for us all. We met a lot of interesting people and interacted with the flight crew that came from assorted backgrounds. One was ex-Rhodesian Air force, one was South African and a couple of others came from the UK having flown for Courtline before it had gone bankrupt and another interesting Captain was an ex test pilot Dickie Martin who flew the Avro 748. One of the VC10 crew members was a local Malawian who became a qualified flight engineer. We got invited to his wedding and most of the guests travelled in a flatbed lorry to his wedding. It was quite funny because Rosemary decided to take group photographs like at our weddings; they had never seen anything like this before. It was smiles all round as they were all ushered in, out and around in groups.

We went to open-air film shows, one being at the Airport Club House, you used to sit there being bitten alive by insects.

Some of the flights we went on were quite eye openers, the flight to Seychelles on a 1-11 was fascinating as you passed over the island of

Aldabra and also Seychelles was at the limit of the BAC 1-11 range. Robbie and I both did trips to Mauritius to bring back passengers because the island had been hit by a cyclone. Robbie went the day before me and it was still very windy out there. A lot of the island was without electricity; I know the hotel I stayed in the day I went was still without power, as we had to walk around with candles. The day I went to Mauritius was quite exciting as you could still see the cloud formation that had formed the cyclone. We had operated both the flights on behalf of Zambia Airways so on both occasions we flew out empty from Blantyre and came back with a full load.

Trevor and I had a few days in Seychelles when the VC10 had reported a broken wing leading edge slat section. We found the actuator and brackets had broken so we had no choice but to call for a team from Gatwick to come out and fix the problem, as we had no spares. The next day as the team of Gatwick engineers Bryan Tilbury, Jim Hook and John Faulkner were arriving we asked if the Airport Restaurant Chef could cook a special meal for them. When they had cleared Customs etc. we led them into the restaurant and the Chef came out with plates of Octopus. You should have seen their faces, they all said sorry Chef have you got any Chicken? When we arrived back in Malawi having made the VC10 serviceable it was nice to be thanked by the Boss of Air Malawi, he was actually waiting at the bottom of the aircraft steps for us.

Once the 6 months was up in June 1975 it was back to Gatwick and pick up where you had left off.

About 3 months later I went back down to Malawi to change an engine on the VC10. The aircraft was retired from Service in 1978 due to costs.

Chapter 47

Back in Hangar 3 it was more Boeing 707 major maintenance; this carried on until 1984 when the 707s left our fleet. We were very sorry to see the end of the 707s as we gained an awful lot of experience working on them.

*Boeing 707 in Hangar 3 on major overhaul, note tail removed and crane starting to remove the engines. When the engines have been removed the aircraft would be jacked up and the landing gear removed. With the engines and tail removed the centre of gravity had shifted a lot so we had to put ballast in the forward hold until the aircraft was stabilised with a nose and tail jack, the tail jack only acted as a steady with all the load sp*read across the main and nose jacks otherwise you could bend the fuselage.

Boeing 707 in Hangar 3 with engines and tail refitted, getting masked up for paint spraying at lunchtime, another smelly afternoon ahead of us. The hangar looks a bit untidy with an engine cowling lying on the floor. As you can see we at that time never had the luxury of dedicated docking so as you can see we had an assortment of different access stands around the hangar.

The final couple of days on a Boeing 707 major maintenance input entailed all the flight control checks and inspections to be carried out, undercarriage retractions, and sometimes weighing the aircraft. When all this was completed we would take the aircraft out of the hangar and start up the engines checking for leaks etc. We would then get clearance to taxi the aircraft to the far end of the runway to what was called "holding point echo" this also was the compass swinging base. We would be down there for 3 to 4 hours completing all the required checks and inspections. If required it also enabled us to do a compass swing at the same time.

We would have a couple of dozen engineers still working in the cabin, they would be finishing off the seats and testing the in-flight entertainment. We would have a couple of urns of hot water in one of the galleys so we could make tea and coffee also some sandwiches on board, it was treated as a day out for the boys.

This was then followed by a test flight and a return to service.

Just a point of interest we had one Boeing 707 on a major check that was a real struggle to get finished, we had been inundated with repairs and were running about two weeks behind schedule. Everyone on the aircraft was getting fed up. The undercarriage had been fitted and the aircraft was on the ground, we had also hung the engines onto the pylons. Mike Gardner, Eric Ludkin and I got together and tried to work out how we could get enthusiasm into the team working on the aircraft. We decided to tow the aircraft out of the hangar and bring it back in nose first and hope this would act as a sign we were getting to the end. It helped a lot but the only down side was that people had been used to working on the aircraft with the tail at the back of the hangar and they were now confronted with the nose at the back of hangar and at times got mixed up with what was left and what was right and which engine was which, one guy was allocated to work on number 4 engine and actually did the job on number 1 engine instead.

On other occasions when we had an overrun we, that's Mike, Eric and Myself would get called up to see Arnold Sheead, he would get all annoyed at the time the aircraft was taking and would always say that the Commercial Department were on his back asking when it was going to be back in service. He sometimes got us to convert the aircraft from a passenger to a freighter configuration and use that as a reason for the delay.

The last 707s left in 1984 (G-AXRS and G-AYEX)

The company was starting to look into wide body aircraft like the Lockheed TriStar, Boeing 747 and the Douglas DC10. Wide body aircraft at that time were becoming much more fashionable, in actual fact we had sent some of the B707 aircraft to Wichita in America to have a wide body EFFECT carried out in the cabin, this was achieved by fitting a different type of overhead locker.

But now most operators were into wide-bodied aircraft that had 2 aisles. We in engineering had a team looking at the three different types of aircraft. At that time the B747 was not practical, the routes we operated did not require four engines, the Tristar looked a good prospect but the ones the company looked at were going to be ex-BEA, however, the Government stepped in and they went to the RAF. So that left the DC10, which at the end of the day was a very good choice.

DC10-30 in Hangar 5 on major maintenance note left hand engine and pylon removed for modifications to the pylon

Hangar 5 was purpose built for the DC10 with the idea that you could if needed get a 747 into the hangar by disconnecting the hangar door mechanism and pushing the doors open manually to their stops. This actually gave you 6" extra clearance on each wind tip so the 747 was towed very slowly into the hangar. When the aircraft was parked there was still about 30 or so feet outside the hangar.

Hangar 5 when it was completed had a mezzanine floor so you could off load all the aircraft seats and galleys and put them straight into the upholstery/seat repair bay.

On the subject of hangars. Hangar 3 had a set of clamshell doors that were fitted on tracks and would close around the tail of the DC10 aircraft on minor maintenance.

Initially the clamshell doors had been installed without any proper locking mechanism apart from two concrete blocks at both ends of the track. This seemed to be satisfactory until we got a very high wind and one of the doors took off along the track and smashed into the concrete block, they were rapidly modified with proper locking mechanisms.

As we all know the Health & Safety at Work Act came into being in 1974 but for us in the hangar it was not an overnight rush out to buy in new equipment. First Frank Lucas who was an ex RAF Crew Chief and a very experienced engineer had worked for us for some time as a tradesman; he was promoted to a new rank of

Equipment Engineer. It was his job to recommend the purchase of new safe equipment for the use of engineering at Gatwick.

Eventually out went the old access stands and Frank brought in more robust items which could conform to the new Safety Laws, we even hired electrical buggies that worked on a scissor principal that you could drive around the hangar yourself standing on a safe and secure platform and raise and lower the buggy as you wished, they were very useful working under the wings. The only thing you had to remember was to plug it into the mains when you had finished otherwise the batteries would go flat.

Frank also brought in at that time a certain amount of mobile staging but all in all we were much better off.

Some of the lads went to Long Beach in California for courses while the rest of us had our courses at Gatwick as Douglas had sent their own Instructors.

The Airframe course was six weeks duration with an awful lot of course note books, these were supplied by the manufactures. When I say note books they were in actual fact all pictures, not a single word anywhere. Each book was about 4" thick (about 100mm) and if I remember right we had about 12 sets each.

The Instructors we had were fun guys; one of them was an ex-marine. One morning he patted himself down and said 'Hey looks like I am out of smokes' then he put his left leg up onto a chair and pulled his trouser leg up to reveal a packet of cigarettes in his socks. He then said 'a good marine always had a smoke hidden somewhere'. The other guy on another occasion when he was talking about the cabin doors whilst pointing at the screen that had a picture of a cabin door on it he said 'you better watch your pinkie when you adjust this part' we all looked at each other, what the heck is he on about, he then held up a hand and wiggled his little finger and said 'you can severely damage it if you are not careful'.

The engine course featuring the General Electric CF6-50 engine was run by our own instructor Dave Campbell and ran for two weeks.

When we took delivery of the DC10 aircraft in 1977 we had signed an agreement with the ATLAS group of companies that included Alitalia, the Italian state airline. The arrangement being that each airline buys a certain major component, for example one company would buy an undercarriage assembly, and another would buy a flying control assembly then each and every operator within the group would have access to this equipment. Our contribution was to be a full set of seven brand new galleys that were tailor made for the ATLAS group of companies, it was a heck of an investment for BCAL bearing in mind we would have no requirement to replace our galleys for at least four years. Then when we found we had some damage to a forward cabin seat track Alitalia said as they are the main structural company within the group that they must come and do the repair themselves, bearing in mind we had been doing seat rack repairs for goodness knows how long, this was the last straw and as far as I know the company got out of the contract one way or another.

As everyone is aware the DC10 had a few serious problems over the years, fortunately we never suffered any of these.

We were told there was one piece of kit we had to buy to enable us to repair any damaged hydraulic pipes, the kit was called a swaging kit. We found a manufacture in Paris, France. Ron Gunner told me to go and have a look at it and if okay we were to order it, this turned out to be one of the most bizarre trips I have ever done. I departed one morning from Gatwick on a 1-11 for Charles de Gaulle Airport, when we landed one of the cabin crew said we have confirmation that you are to be fast tracked through the terminal. I was told I would be meeting a guy holding up a board. When the passenger door was opened I was met by a traffic chap who said follow me, we whizzed through all the arrival procedures and before I knew it I was in the arrivals hall. Now if there was one chap holding up a board there must have been 50. Anyhow I met the right guy who then rushed off with me and got into his car. He said would you like a quick tour round Paris and I said that would be nice, we proceeded to do that at break neck speed and I do not remember much at all about the journey as no sooner had we started we appeared to be at the factory. At the factory they had laid on a demonstration of the equipment, which was quite impressive, as it did everything we would require. He then said we would go out for a quick lunch and as my French is non-existent I asked him to order for me. The meal arrived complete with a bottle of wine and I started to eat what was a very nice meal, however, on the plate was some very small green things which I thought were very small peas so I took a mouth full of them only to find that they were some spicy very hot something or other, I could hardly talk and my mouth felt like it was on fire and even a glass of wine would not cool things down. The day concluded with him returning me to the Airport followed by an uneventful flight home and him receiving a purchase order for one kit. That kit stayed in Stores for the duration of the DC10 operation and I cannot remember it ever being used.

When we got into the major maintenance programme on the DC10 we would have to remove all the seats, carpets, toilets, all seven galleys and all the floorboards so that we could carry out inspection of the structure. At that time we had a Douglas representative a lady called Mrs Margaret Post, she asked me if I would walk her around the aircraft so that she could see what we were doing and what we had found on our inspection. We eventually walked into the stripped out cabin and I happened to mention that we had found some corrosion under the forward toilet floor, she looked at me and said "well I guess that is the place we will find corrosion if we are going to find any" I must admit I felt a bit of an idiot and did not know how to respond to her but just said to her lets walk on down the cabin.

We did have one fuel system problem with the DC10 that was quite a difficult item to fix because it was associated with a couple of valves out near the wing tips in the very narrow part of the fuel tank. So the rep Mrs Post set up a conference call with Douglas the manufactures at about 17:00 hrs one evening, there must have been about half a dozen of us around the table at Gatwick. The telephones were on speaker so we could all hear what was being said, so we explained the problem to the people in America and they responded but did not seem to be getting our point. All they kept saying was well change the valves, out of frustration I remember saying I wish I could talk to the chap that designed the system, somebody on the other end said you are actually talking to him WHOOPS!!

We had some interesting times with the DC10s. We sold one of them to Continental Airlines from America; we had a small group of engineers from Continental looking over what we were doing. We had to convert the aircraft to Federal Aviation Authority (FAA) so that we complied with their requirements.

None of the Continental Airways chaps had been to the UK before, they had hired a car and I asked them one day how they were getting on with our road system and they all said once you could find your way off a roundabout it is not too bad, what they did not understand was how you can follow a road sign especially in rural areas and then all of a sudden you never see a sign anymore.

We almost fell foul to the FAA Inspector on completion of the cabin, we had fitted all the cabin seats and seat belts as to how we operated them but he wanted all the aisle seats to have the belts fitted the opposite way round, that way the heavy part of the seat buckle would not catch anybody on the knee resulting in an injury whereby the company would be sued, he told us he would issue a piece of paper to that effect and if we did not comply the FAA would hit us with a fine.

The aircraft had an air test on a Saturday morning. The crew asked if some of us would like to go up on the test, we had about six volunteers including myself. What you have got to remember now is this was before flight deck doors were locked because all six of us piled into the flight deck for the duration of the flight.

Another contact we had was with Air Florida. We did a few service checks in the hangar on their DC10s. Each aircraft was supported by its own paperwork, inspection sheets etc. prepared in Florida and dispatched with the aircraft. We had the occasional FAA Inspector in the hangar and found they could ask some very awkward questions; one being you are just about to certify this aircraft to return to service, how do you know all the relevant paperwork is correct? Fortunately we had thought of this and could answer him correctly.

I must say the best part of the Air Florida contract was the bags of peanuts they carried for the passengers, they were Almond flavour and the best peanuts any of us had ever tasted and quite a few packets were consumed off the aircraft.

Our real surprise contract was with the United States Air Force the contract was to service three of their KC10 tanker aircraft (in-flight refuelling).

Before we received any of the aircraft some of the USAF staff came over to visit, the Colonel in charge was horrified with the amount of doors, corridors and exits we had in Hangar 5, he said it was more like a rabbit warren and we would have to close some of these off. We would also have to rope off all around the aircraft whilst it was in the hangar and issue special passes to only the staff allocated to the aircraft. He then told us once we started work on the aircraft because they were operational aircraft and could be required at any point in time we would have to tailor the work load into what he called time to serviceability slots. This was arranged in 6-hour increments starting from 24 hours working down to zero so that meant if he came up to us and said the aircraft is required in 18 hours we had to make sure it was ready for immediate release to service. This all felt a little bit over the top to us but that was what they wanted.

The first aircraft arrived one evening at about 19:00, we were only told it was on its way, they wanted us to have a 45 gallon empty oil drum available also a tractor on standby at the hangar, everything was very hush hush, the aircraft arrived, taxied straight to the hangar, we had to have the hangar doors open, the tractor hooked up to the aircraft. When the crew got off the aircraft the Captain said where is the empty drum, we showed him and he put all of his mission papers in the drum and set fire to it all and we were told to get the aircraft into the hangar and doors closed within five minutes so as to conform to their 'minimum' exposure time.

One of the three aircraft we had was painted in a camouflage colour and their Engineering Chief told us to be very careful because that sort of paint marked very easily. When I told them we had a couple of resident pigeons in the roof of Hangar 5 he was not very happy, he said their droppings would really mess up the paintwork so we told him they only roost up in the rafters on the left hand side of the hangar so we will put polythene sheeting over the top of the wing before we go home. What happened the two pigeons either had an argument or something or other because in the morning they had moved over and messed the right hand wing, this had never ever happened before so we frantically tried to clean it all up before he turned up for work.

We by that time late 1970s early 80s had gained quite a lot of experience on the DC10s, however, we got completely baffled by one of the USAF guys saying 'I put a bag of the screws behind the California door' now what on earth was he on about? It turned out that when you walked into the cabin via the left hand forward passenger door just to your left was a small cupboard door we had never thought of it before but the door was actually shaped in the outline of California hence another example of common language.

Another example of our expertise with the USAF was that on one of the aircraft one of our engineers found a damaged compressor fan blade that needed changing so with no further ado we contacted Caledonian Air Motive in Scotland, they were our own engine overhaul division and asked them if we send a blade up to you could you replace it with one of the same weight and balance, they told us it would be no problem, so the blade was removed and put onto our next BAC 1-11 service to Glasgow and a replacement bade was sent down to Gatwick. Night shift guys fitted the new blade. In the morning we told the USAF Engineering Chief what we had done. He was taken aback as he knew nothing about what had taken place, he told us we should have let him know as he would then had told his boss who in turn would had gone up the chain of command and he said it would have gone all the way to the Pentagon and it would have taken four to five days to get permission and that would have taken the aircraft out of operations and they would have to had flown another aircraft over to the UK. He was amazed we had done it in less than 12 hours. He was well impressed with BCAL Engineering.

We never heard or saw anything of the USAF after the three aircraft had been worked on, overall it was a very unique and rewarding experience and I must say at this point one of the main organisers in the hangar was Tony Barber. Tony is ex-Laker Airways and was a very good organiser and engineer.

Tony along with a few others joined BCAL after the collapse of Laker Airways in 1982.

Chapter 48

After Laker's folded Ron Gunner and myself went up to their hangar to see if there was any equipment we needed and could buy. It was a horrible feeling standing in the hangar that was now empty with no staff or aircraft when you consider all the hours the staff worked to make a success of the company and at the end of the day it was all for nothing.

We took on the ex-Laker DC10-10 aircraft as Cal Air, which formed a charter wing for BCAL. We had the first aircraft in Hangar 3 being serviced and brought up to speed with BCALs maintenance schedule.

At that time when an aircraft was in the hangar for a 'service check' whereby it had its maintenance work planned to comply with the maintenance schedule, all the work carried out was certified by qualified engineers and at the end of the inspection when all the paperwork was completed a senior qualified engineer approved by the CAA would sign the last piece of paper so as to return the aircraft to service. In the hangar at that time I was one of those people, however, when we had almost completed the maintenance of the first ex-Laker DC10-10 we realised that I could not sign the aircraft back to service because our approval only covered the BCAL DC10-30 aircraft.

How did we get out of this hole we found ourselves in, a quick telephone call to the CAA was on the cards. At that time we had working for us two ex-Laker Engineers Dick Plowes and Roy Gardener, now Roy whilst employed by Lakers and being of senior rank held the approval by the CAA to certify it back to service. But whilst employed by BCAL he was only a Supervisor rank and therefore could not carry out this duty.

The telephone call to the CAA resulted in them instructing Roy to ask me the differences between the two types of aircraft and for him then to reply back to the CAA and when they were happy I was then granted authorisation and that is how we got out of the problem.

Now a few stories about three lads from Lakers.

First Roy Gardner, we were in Hangar 3 one day working on a Boeing 707 when Roy had a telephone call and when he came back he said to me that was a funny old conversation, an ex-Laker Captain who knew Roy well had said that Richard Branson wants to set up an Airline and we were wondering if you would like to be Chief Engineer which Roy accepted and off he went.

Dick Plowes was ex-Laker Quality Control Engineer and he joined BCAL on Quality Control. I remember Dick did not like flying that much, three of us Dick, John Stuckle from Planning and myself went to Cairo. We arrived at Heathrow and Dick had to have a couple of drinks before we boarded an Egypt Air Airbus A300 aircraft to Cairo. When we arrived we were told the 707 aircraft that we were to inspect was over near the scrap yard, this was quite a way away from the main Airport and we had to be transported all the time. The idea was that we looked at the aeroplane with a view to flying it to Gatwick for a major check, but when we looked around it we found it was so corroded that we told them just to push it back into the scrap yard.

John's success was to clear all the paperwork and he came back to us one morning holding a set of keys in his hand and said I have been given the key to the European Toilet, anyone who had been out there knows what I am talking about. Dick wrote up a report back in the hotel sitting in the corridor under an emergency light as the hotel had a power cut.

Finally Rick Axby. I think after leaving the RAF Rick worked for nearly all the Airlines at Gatwick and had a fist full of qualifications. Rick came to us on Quality Control, he was well known for his speed about the hangar. His retirement presentation was an engine blade mounted on a stand with flame coming out of the base. I saw Rick a little while ago and he still has his beloved Morris Minor car.

Chapter 49

BCAL then ordered the Airbus A310; we had courses on the aircraft at Gatwick and went to Toulouse in France for simulator training. The training was for engine running and we had to carry this out over-night, as the simulator was used daytime for flight crews.

BCAL did not operate the aircraft very long as it did not meet the route requirements we had at the time and quite frankly I cannot ever remember working on it.

We then ventured into the world of the Boeing 747, once again the courses were held at Gatwick. Ron Thaxter and Mick Williams were the two main guys associated with the 747 when they were introduced into the service.

We did a major mod programme on the Boeing 747 that took it out of service for 22 days. The mod was to stiffen the forward cabin floor beams. Dave Lear and I were assigned to plan the work and sort out the complex mod kit and lay it out on the hangar floor in some sort of order. Prior to doing this Dave and I took a trip to Heathrow and spoke to the British Airways Planners about the mod, they thought we were daft, as being a small company taking on such a task, as they were not going to modify their aircraft until a later date.

We undertook the task in Hangar 3 and jacked the aircraft up off the ground bearing in mind the tail stuck out of the hangar some 30 – 40 ft. and we had to be mindful of the wind speeds across the front of the hangar as you could get an eddying effect over the hangar roof where the wind would just swirl around the front of the hangar.

We were watched during this mod by representatives from different airlines EL AL being one of them and a couple of people from America; they all thought we were brave but foolhardy to take on the work.

However, we completed the work on time to everybody's satisfaction.

We took on another big chunk of work mainly Hapag Lloyds A300 Airbus that required a major check. By this time BCAL had acquired Laker's old hangar and it was now called Hangar 6.

Most of the inspection work was carried out by ex-Laker supervisors over a period of time that had been employed by us as they had Airbus experience to name a few of them Bob Selmes, Sandy Sanderson and Steve Brand. Please forgive me for forgetting other names; it fell to

Eric Ludkin, John Stuckle and I to oversee the work. It was a bit of a challenge and our first venture into composite structures, we had to use the services of an outside company that specialised in non-destructive testing work.

One particular repair caused us a little headache, which was a repair to the forward left hand doorframe; we submitted the damage report to Airbus in Toulouse whose design/stress department called up a permanent repair. We ordered the material through our purchasing department, after a few days our purchasing department told us they could not get the particular material so we contacted Airbus and they said we are very sorry but we had called up material that as yet was not on the market place so they then gave us an alternative to use.

We even had a situation where we needed certain spares urgently to keep the aircraft on schedule, but the cross channel lorry drivers had gone on strike so we could not get the spares, we had to resort to hiring a helicopter to pick up what we needed.

We had within BCAL a good understanding with our purchasing department; we used to invite them over to the hangar so that they could see what we were doing, because they did not understand the sequence of work we were undertaking. The aircraft might not be scheduled to be completed for another three weeks but we needed certain spares to keep the work flowing, this practice worked very well and they constantly phoned us to say they can't get this or do that so will a couple of days delay cause you any problems!

Chapter 50

As engineering got larger we introduced a Control Centre away from the hangar, this was located on the top floor of Hangar 5, engineers from different departments manned it and they could talk to the hangar, to the ramp and to operations. It was staffed by the likes of Hugh Cowan, Roger Olden, Gordon Harrison and others I have once again forgotten.

There is a good saying that goes something like "when you go up the ladder be careful as you never know who you will meet on the way down".

Mick Williams joined BCAL from the RAF. Fred Ansell who was the Hangar Foreman at the time came up to me first thing on a Monday morning and said we have a new starter and he can work for you on the Boeing 707. Mick and I had quick introductions and I put Mick to work in the cabin doing repairs. Mick at that time unbeknown to me was studying for an Open University exam. He was a nice guy he got on well with everyone and Mick rapidly grew within engineering and as I said earlier he became a key player on the Boeing 747 and regarding the saying about the ladder Mick became my Senior Manager when British Airways took us over. The last I heard of Mick he had become

Engineering Manager of GO Airline, BAs budget Airline at the time.

Another strange thing, once again on a Monday morning I was coming out of the cabin of a DC10 in Hangar 5 when a young apprentice came over to me and said he had been told to report to Hangar 5 and work for me on a DC10.   His surname was Baker, once again I have forgotten his first name but he told me he was the son of Bill Baker who helped to train me way back in the 50s. Bill was the chap who called everything 'EF' and I felt as though I had gone full circle.

Talking of apprentices after Buck Ryan who was the Apprentice Supervisor who had retired, Eric Ludkin and I for about three years interviewed the young people who wanted to become apprentices.

All in all they were all a great bunch of youngsters but unfortunately we only had a few places each year to fill so sadly we had to turn quite a few away. One of which I remember was an inventor of mechanical things, he brought in with him some of the things he had designed and made. We had to tell him you cannot invent things working on aircraft, in fact you will find yourself working in freight holds undoing screws removing panels refitting panels and working on toilets etc. He said don't worry I will think of a better way of doing these jobs. I often wonder what he is doing now.

Another guy came all the way up from Hong Kong. We Eric and I had a set of questions that we would ask each one so that it was fair to everybody. One of the questions was "okay if on take-off the aircraft has a bird strike what would happen to the engine", we slightly altered this question by saying, "okay on your flight from Hong Kong what would have happened due to a bird strike". He sat there for a moment and then said nothing would happen as we have no sea birds in Hong Kong due to pollution, that rather threw a spanner in the works and we both sort of stuttered out the next question.

My favourite memory was of a young lady immaculately dressed, long hair, painted fingernails, the whole works. We said to her now if we offer you a job you will have to put your hair up in a net for safety, your finger nails will get dirty and chipped and you will be wearing thick soled safety shoes. We then asked her how do you feel about that? All she said was "great that's what I want". I like to think all the youngsters taken on by BUA and BCAL have had enjoyable careers but the frightening thing to me is that some of the early entries have now joined the retired ranks, which makes me feel very old.

We had one lad Jim Wilson who went on to become a Captain and I still see him occasionally. We had two lads who thought they were not earning enough money and left and went working on the roads doing repairs etc. And I will always remember Carl Traynor, I asked him one day what his ambition was and he said; I want your job. In latter days with BA he had reached that position and I said to him, how do you like it now? I won't repeat his answer.

.

Chapter 51

At some time in the late 1980s we had closed Hangar 1 as the M.T Section was using it. The aircraft maintenance was then spread between Hangars 3, 5 and 6. It was decided that we needed to upgrade the BAC 1-11 500 fleet to give them a wide-bodied cabin appearance and to embody an auto land modification. The wide-bodied appearance would be done in the same sort of fashion as we had done on the Boeing 707s by fitting different shape overhead lockers. At this time we had sold the 200 series 1-11s to Pacific Express and we just had an expanded fleet of 500 series aircraft.

To accomplish the planned modification programme on the 1-11, which was to include the complete auto land system, required us to take back from the Motor Transport Section, Hangar 1, for us to use as an aircraft hangar again.

Ron Gunner was to be the Maintenance Superintendent and I was to be Foreman. We were allocated staff from each hangar so that we had our own dedicated team, as the mod programme was complicated and very time consuming.

I must digress at this point just to explain that Bill Richardson who was the Engineering

Director had now retired and we had a new Engineering Director Norman Jackson who had just left the RAF, I cannot remember what rank he was but it was pretty high up, he brought with him three ex RAF Officers, one to run the Ramp, one for the Hangar (Martin Hurst) and one for the Maintenance Control Centre. The first thing that happened once the RAF chaps had settled in was to get all the equipment painted blue and where all the equipment was parked in the hangar the floor was painted yellow.

My personal belief is that none of these ex RAF guys really got to grips with Civil Aviation and the way it operated, Martin might have been the exception but I remember one Saturday morning he was Duty Manager and he came into Hangar 5 where we were fitting a lot of freight hold panels and asked if he could help in anyway as he was bored just walking around. He spent quite a few hours winding screws into freight hold panels and seemed to quite enjoy it, less for the lads to do.

Back to the 1-11 mod programme; we had reached a point where the mods were complete and the aircraft was being readied for a test flight. The Chief 1-11 pilot Captain John Duncan had spent a fair bit of time with us in the hangar seeing what we were doing.

We cleared all the paperwork for the aircraft and prepared it for flight, now when you embody major mods you invalidate the Certificate of Airworthiness so you cannot return the aircraft to service in the normal way. What we had to do was once all the supervisors had cleared all their paperwork one person would sign what was called a 'blood chit' which would say that the aircraft was fit to fly.

It was about 18:30 on a summers evening that we were ready for the test flight and the ex RAF Officer who was in charge of the maintenance control centre came into the hangar and asked how we were getting on. I told him I was just going to sign the 'blood chit' he then got completely confused by saying how can the aircraft fly because it has no C of A (Certificate of Airworthiness), it took quite a bit of explaining and he eventually walked away shaking his head.

The flight went okay and it took a few more flights to enable the aircraft to regain its C of A. After the test flying and everybody was happy it then became a complete auto land aircraft.

After the first aircraft was completed I got called back into Hangar 5 onto DC10 major maintenance until the British Airways take over. Ron Gunner retired and the BAC 1-11 mod

340

programme soldiered on until all the aircraft were complete.

One other aircraft we had that is worth a mention was an Affretair DC8 that operated through Salisbury in Rhodesia. The aircraft came into the hangar for modifications and repairs. There were two engineers from Affretair that came into the hangar with us, they told us stories of what the aircraft had been used for and I need to say at this time that the aircraft was a complete freighter. Some of the stories they told us I would not repeat here.

One of BCALs strength was its Commercial, Sales and PR Staff Departments.

We often saw people being shown around the hangars either daytime or evening, we had on one occasion a group of blind children being taken around the hangars and you saw grown up engineers rushing over to see if they could help in taking the children around. I always remember one little boy standing by the main wheel of one of the aircraft and feeling with his hands the top of the wheel and saying "it's as tall as me".

Our security boss must originally have had a military background because we would get a message from him saying he would be bringing a group of "friends" around. Could we have a couple of engineers to show them over the aircraft? These guys always arrived in civvies, and we quickly figured out who they were because all they asked us was where does this hatch way lead to and where can I cut into the aeroplane with an axe, they used to climb all over the aircraft.

Advertising was a massive boost to the airline. We often had film crews around the aircraft and on one occasion we had Peter Cooke and Dudley Moore making a film.

Then along came the TV adverts one of which I got to play a small part crouching behind the nose wheel of a 707 pretending to be taking out the nose landing gear safety pin.

Now this leads to a funny story. One day back at Gatwick one of our engineers Burt Charlesworth came across the hangar to me having arrived back from Nairobi where he had been Station Engineer, and he said he had a lousy day in Nairobi on a turnaround of a 707 when an engine driven hydraulic pump packed up, he then had to change it, now these pumps were a right pig to change, Burt got the job done and departed the aircraft. In the evening he and his wife decided to go the cinema to get away from it all. He said we were sitting in the seats, the adverts started to come on and the first thing I saw was your blessed face on the screen, I just could not get away from work.

There are so many engineers who made BCAL such a success, that to mention them all would be impossible.

As I have spoken mainly about engine and airframe staff I must mention a few of our avionic lads, Roger Olden and Ron Francis who did sterling work getting us fitted out with uniforms much against the managements wishes at the time. Brian Gladman and Brian Gawn two really outstanding avionic fitters. Geoff Wright who took a lot of stick from Ron Gunner and myself when he first got promoted as supervisor. Dick Conway who would sort out any problem for you then we have the two radio guys Roy Ward and Ron Holt.

One thing we could always rely on with the avionic staff was when we had to move heavy equipment or push on the hangar doors they would all disappear.

I almost forgot Eddie Jones, I don't think anyone could forget Eddie, I notice he is even on the BCAL website.

PART 4

British Airways
1988 to 2005

Chapter 52

My sole purpose of writing this book had been to capture events that happened back in the 'good old days', some say 'not so good old days'.

The late 1980's saw the demise of BCAL, Dan Air and Laker. All gone in body but not in spirit, they and other Airlines from what used to be called The Independent Airlines still live on through websites, reunions and memorabilia but mainly through ex-staff members' own memories.

Therefore the latter years of my career following the take-over by British Airways will suffice to say, some people enjoyed it whilst others could not leave quickly enough, many for the simple reason that they didn't want to work for a very large Airline.

I believe the takeover by BA went as well as could be expected when you consider the difficulties they had in merging BEA and BOAC together. I, along with others spent quite a lot of time learning the differences of operation between BA and BCAL and considering the previous merger between the two corporations had taken place quite a while ago you often still found pockets of employees still wishing they were either BOAC or BEA, it just goes to prove that although we accept change we find it difficult to let go of the past, I knew engineers in BCAL, one comes to mind immediately who enjoyed the RAF and didn't like his current employer BUA, but then when BCAL took over BUA he thought BUA was the best thing ever. Just the way of the world I Suppose!!

During the latter stages of my career I personally had at least 17 years with British Airways with which I learned an awful lot of different skills and had a varied career path ranging from Engineering Maintenance to assisting with the introduction of business management within the engineering department. Captain Mike Jeffreys headed up the introduction of business management at that time; he was from the B747 fleet (Mike was a real gentleman). This role also encompassed working alongside Engineering Finance.

I completed my career on 30 April 2005 in the Engineering Department, monitoring aircraft performance and various other bits and pieces.

One thing I will always be grateful to BA for are the Long Service Award Schemes. During my time with BA I had my 35, 45 and 50 year Awards. On my 35-year service my wife and I were invited to the Company's Shareholders AGM, followed by a lunch in a Hotel on Park Lane. We also had a dinner at a The Old House restaurant in Smallfield and were able to invite 3 guests along with my boss Fred Whetnell.

The icing on the cake must be my 45 years' service in 2000 and being awarded a pair of return tickets from LHR to JFK on Concorde for my wife and I. Sadly we had to wait until May 2002 due to the Air France crash in July 2000 owing to the aircraft fleet being modified.

My last award at 50 years was lunch in the Boardroom at Waterside for my wife and myself along with Alan McDonald who was then Engineering Director, Rod Eddington Chief Executive Officer and Fred Whetnell my boss.

The whole of the week Fred told me that he was available to take my wife and I anywhere we wanted to go, he drove us to Waterside and back home.

My last day I was presented with lots of gifts plus a DVD that Mike Keely had put together that went through all the aircraft I had been associated with during my career and also high lights of world events over the 50 years, this was all set to music. Mike did a marvellous job producing this and it is a treasured possession of mine. Last but not least, the year I retired in 2005, BA Engineering presented for the first time an award called "The Person Of The Year" and I was lucky enough to win the award, I am not sure if it was because they were glad to see the back of me or hopefully because of what I had actually achieved and contributed to engineering?

My desk was littered with gold glitter stuff with 50 years. The day of the presentation they even managed to get my wife and daughter into the presentation unbeknown to me.

Another thing Mike did that caught me out was one day we were talking and he had a video and a microphone recording what I was saying, this he put on the end of the DVD and also got in touch with the editor of the BA Engineering magazine who ran an article on me entitled "An Historic Career".

Although I am now retired and enjoying my life with my family and horses I still see aircraft taking off and landing on a daily basis as we live under the flight path into LGW, purely by design of course! Gatwick is very busy these days and when I look up every time an aircraft fly's overhead my wife says "it's only an aeroplane Rog" (she does not call them planes and small aircraft she calls old bangers), I tell her it's an Airbus or a Boeing going over she just shakes her head and walks away laughing. I could at one time tell the difference through the engine sound but as time marches on sounds change. It only seems like yesterday you could look up and see a BCAL DC10 or a BUA VC10 thundering away and of course before that the work horses of days gone by the Viscounts and Dakotas of Transair, what memories I have. I am fortunate to have my company pension and staff travel perk, which luckily for me lasts until my 115th birthday (don't think I will make that last trip, but you never know). So, in my own mind I am still involved in aviation and if I had a chance I'd do it all again. It's funny but talking to people who trained me at that time all say they had the best years of aviation, my generation say they had the best, I guess it will always be like that.

Before we close the hangar doors for the last time, just a few thoughts cross my mind. In my career I have seen Piston engines and jet powered aircraft also to include Concorde and bearing in mind only 52 years before I started work the Wright Brothers in America made that historic first flight on the 17th December 1903, flying for 12 seconds at a height of approximately 10 ft and speed of 6.8 miles per hour. Now 14 years after my retirement Qantas in Australia are looking to fly a twin jet Boeing 787 Dreamliner non-stop from Australia to London with over 200 passengers on board. What will the next generation be able to say I wonder? Will we be back into Supersonic???

Chapter 53

In Conclusion

Looking back over time the South side of LGW had at one time or another a collection of purpose built buildings for Airlines that had housed, flight kitchens, ground support electrical workshop, property maintenance staff, cabin service training rooms, seat bay for the configuration gang, admin staff office block and even a sports and social club house.

We had 6 Hangars plus the wooden hangar now all the buildings and hangars have been bulldozed to the ground except Hangar 6 the old Laker hangar.

The Dunlop tyre company at one time had a building on the South side that's also gone.

Various people over the years said I was silly and should have gone to other companies to gain experience. The way I viewed it was that I met a lot of people who came from other airlines and I have listed below are most but not all of the aircraft I have been involved with in my 50 Years:

- Douglas DC3, DC4, DC6, DC8, DC10-10 and DC10-30 plus US KC10 Tankers.

- Vickers Viscounts type 708, 736, 804, 831 and 833.
- Vickers Viking and Valetta.
- Bristol Britannia types 307, 309 and 313.
- Handley Page Dart Herald and Hermes.
- Cessna 310
- Avro Anson
- Scottish Aviation Twin Pioneer
- Bristol type 170 Freighter
- Lockheed Constellation
- BAC 1-11 type 201,400 and 500
- Vickers VC10
- Boeing 707-320C, B737, 747, 757, 767 and 777
- Airbus A300, A310

A real variety of aircraft when I remember interviewing a tradesman at LHR for a job at LGW he told me he had worked on civil aircraft for 14 years and in that time had only worked on a B747 in the cabin.

My last thoughts: After 50 years and one week and some 26 aircraft types later I would like to finish the book with the words old Titch who trained me said when I asked him what he loved about aircraft and airlines. He told me "Roger aviation is a glorious uncertainty, where what you plan today has changed by tomorrow". How right he was and if all of you who read this have as wonderful a life in aviation as I have had, you won't go far wrong.

This last paragraph is an extract from the British Airways Leading Edge Magazine dated April/May 2005, which described my career as "An Historic Career".

The end.